Critical Guides to Spanish Texts

D0264456

15 Lazarillo de Tormes

Critical Guides to Spanish Texts

EDITED BY J.E. VAREY, A.D. DEYERMOND AND C. DAVIES

Lazarillo de Tormes

A CRITICAL GUIDE

Second Edition

Alan Deyermond

Professor of Spanish,
Queen Mary and Westfield College, London

Grant & Cutler Ltd
in association with Tamesis Books Ltd

ISBN 0 7293 0352 7

First edition 1975
Second edition 1993

I.S.B.N. 84-599-3305-9

DEPÓSITO LEGAL: V. 211-1993

Printed in Spain by
Artes Gráficas Soler, S.A., Valencia
for
GRANT & CUTLER LTD
55-57 GREAT MARLBOROUGH STREET, LONDON W1V 2AY

Contents

to Ruth

Preface

This book was written in 1974-75, and has been out of print for some years. That is my fault, not the publisher's. I had promised a rewritten second edition, and began work on it in good time, but my chronic inability to limit my commitments delayed completion for longer than even a tolerant publisher could bear. The present edition, therefore, consists of the text and bibliography of the first edition, with this new Preface and a Supplementary Bibliography, which should bring the book sufficiently up to date for the needs of most readers. The unusually large number of items in the Supplementary Bibliography (which is nevertheless rigorously selective) reflects the extent and quality of work on the picaresque novel in general, and *Lazarillo de Tormes* in particular, since 1975. There are items in the original bibliography that I should not now include: *13* is superseded by *60*, and *35* by *56*; *34* is one of the studies collected in *100*. (*43*, however, is not superseded by *116*: although the author has changed his mind, *43* remains an important — and, I believe, largely valid — interpretation of *LT*.) And there are items which, although they have not been superseded by their authors' later work, and although they were once very useful, have probably served their purpose and are no longer needed by most readers of *LT*: *5*, *15*, *17*, *21*, *24*, *30*, *31*. Where the scope of a work listed in the Supplementary Bibliography is not clearly indicated by its title, I have added an explanatory line or two.

The vigour of recent *Lazarillo* criticism and scholarship has contributed to the delay in producing this second edition: all of the books and articles that are listed, and some that are not, need to be taken into account, so that in a rewritten version of this Guide hardly a page could escape without some addition or modification. The articles collected in the volumes by Francisco Rico (*100*) and

Antonio Vilanova (*114*), the series of articles by George A. Shipley (*106-10*), Harry Sieber's monograph on language (*111*), Víctor García de la Concha's careful reappraisals (*87*), and Francisco Rico's introduction to his edition of *LT* (*60*) are of special importance. The brief account that follows is intended to be indicative, not exhaustive; it will at least give the reader a starting-point for evaluating the opinions that I express in the chapters of this Guide. Books and articles within each group are mentioned in chronological order of publication.

CHAPTER 1. For genre, all the new studies on the picaresque (*47-58*) are obviously important; also, Marina Scordilis Brownlee (*68*) looks at the implications of the two early sequels; Antonio Gómez-Moriana (*75*: 81-103) relates *LT* to Inquisition confession documents (cf. *79*); and Francisco Rico (*100-01*) deals with a variety of aspects. Rico's work (*100*) is also important for *LT*'s bibliographical history. The book's reception is studied by Maxime Chevalier (*71*), Horst Baader's study of anonymous Golden-Age literature (*65*) clarifies *LT*'s generic position, and Dalai Brenes Carrillo (*67*) offers a new candidate for authorship, a question that few scholars have tried to resolve (despite Paul Julian Smith's statement (*112*: 98) that 'Critics have always tried to identify a particular author').

CHAPTER 2. The protagonist's relation to society, and its implications, have been discussed in a dozen studies, some Marxist but most not, all of them illuminating in their different ways. Julio Rodríguez-Puértolas (*102*) sees *LT* as a picture of, among other things, the vulnerability of Charles V's imperial Spain, and soon afterwards L.J. Woodward (*119*) sees Lazarillo's aim of 'salir a buen puerto' as characteristic of a capitalist mentality. Javier Herrero (*91*) links the birth of the picaresque novel with Renaissance controversies on charity, and Augustin Redondo (*98*) similarly looks at the social problems underlying the debate on paupers and beggars. M.J. Woods (*118*) cites documents condemning liaisons between priests and married women, and other documents on water-sellers and town criers, to show that moral judgments on the protagonist may be more difficult than has been supposed. In a different approach that merits further development, José María Alegre (*62*) looks at the role of women in the book. John Beverley (*66*) returns to the idea of Lazarillo's life as representative of early capitalism. José Antonio Maravall's linking of the picaresque to social history (*52*) is useful, though he gives relatively little attention to the sixteenth century. George A. Shipley (*110*) considers in detail the business activities of one of Lázaro's masters and Lázaro's part in them, while Anne J. Cruz (*76*) takes a more general view of the problems, and Antonio Vilanova (*114*: 125-236) discusses the theme of hunger and the corrupting effect of Lazarillo's training.

CHAPTER 3. The question of Erasmian and related influences has been the most discussed, with Woodward (*119*) arguing for an *alumbrado* ideology in the work, Thomas Hanrahan (*88*) maintaining that some elements reflect Lutheran, not just Erasmian, doctrines, and Terence O'Reilly (*95*) and Vilanova (*114*: 237-79) offering fresh evidence of Erasmian influence (Vilanova concentrates on Tratado 3, in which he notes parallels to various works of Erasmus). There is probably more to the links between *LT* and reformist movements than I thought when I wrote this Guide, though it is still difficult to discern exact correspondences with any one set of doctrines. Manuel Ferrer Chivite (*81*) returns to the question of a *converso* origin of the work. Two contrasting studies, which both look at possible parodies of religious elements, are provided by Bruce W. Wardropper (*116*; cf. *95*) and Javier Herrero (*89*).

CHAPTER 4. Margit Frenk (*83*) examines the narrative technique of Tratado 1. Aldo Ruffinatto's two-volume book (*103*) applies the techniques of semiotic and structuralist criticism to large- and small-scale structures, sometimes in too abstract a way, though providing many stimulating insights. Louis Combet (*73*) adopts the same approach as Frenk (*83*), though taking it further by studying just one episode of Tratado 1. Víctor García de la Concha (*87*) offers a more general view of questions of structure, and Frenk (*85*) also broadens her focus by considering the relevance of Axel Olrik's 'Law of Three', a question that had earlier been investigated by Fernando Lázaro Carreter (*26*). Finally, O'Reilly (*96*) accepts the idea of a discontinuity in the structure of *LT* but accounts for it differently

from the critics who had placed the break at the end of Tratado 3: he
argues that Tratado 5, a late addition, changed the structure.

CHAPTER 5. Style (apart from imagery) has been discussed in
different ways: Edmond Cros (*74*) looks at links between semantics
and social structures, while Elsa Dehennin (*78*) distinguishes
between two kinds of language. Harry Sieber's book (*111*) gives
more extensive consideration to these and other questions. Edward
H. Friedman (*86*), on the other hand, is more interested in ambiguity,
as is García de la Concha (*87*). Malcolm K. Read (*97*) returns in part
to Sieber's approach, though differing from him on the implications
of *LT*'s use of language. Antonio Gómez-Moriana (*75*: 21-79) sees a
parodic relation between that language and ritual discourse, while
Emilio Martínez Mata (*93*) considers the question of realistic representation.

CHAPTER 6. Imagery has attracted the attention of only three
critics, though all three have made important contributions: Herrero
(*89, 90*) by analysing two groups of images, Sieber (*111*: 48-57; cf.
113) by studying the images of Tratado 4, and Shipley (*106*) by
doing the same for Tratado 6. All of them have been concerned not
with similes and metaphors but with a different and very important
type of image: the object that is as much a part of the narrative as
any of the characters, but that also has a symbolic function.
Inevitably, there is a risk that some of these analyses may go further
than the context warrants, so it is a pity that these fundamental
contributions to *LT* criticism have not produced the interpretative
debate for which their authors hoped.

CHAPTER 7. Lázaro as narrator and protagonist has attracted
more attention than any other aspect of the work. Wardropper (*116*)
revises the views that he expressed in *43*, and Baader (*65*), as we
have seen, sets in its context the problem of a fictional first-person
narrator in an anonymous work. Much of Sieber's book (*111*) is
concerned with Lázaro as narrator, and he has interesting ideas on
Vuestra Merced's relation to 'el caso' (cf. *64*). Woods (*118*), as we
have also seen, cautions against moral judgments on the protagonist
(is it possible that, in judging those who make moral judgments, he
has fallen into the trap that he has signposted?). His conclusion had

been reached by other critics from different starting-points (see p.94, below). Alfonso Rey (*55*) looks fruitfully at problems of narrative point of view, agreeing in general terms with the views of Rico (*56*). Douglas M. Carey (*69*) and Maxime Chevalier (*72*) look afresh at two aspects of the protagonist, and Colbert I. Nepaulsingh (*94*) argues against the view that the adult Lázaro is a hypocrite. Frenk (*84*) reassesses the author/narrator/character relation, while Georgina Sabat de Rivers (*105*) stresses the contrast between the character's failure and the narrator's success. Friedman (*86*) is interested in narrator and point of view, with the ambiguity that results, questions that also preoccupy García de la Concha (*87*). Wardropper (*117*) returns to the issue of hypocrisy, and a pair of articles by Shipley (*107-08*) deal with this and other charges against Lázaro. Robert Archer (*64*) offers a new and attractive hypothesis (on which, inevitably, it is impossible to reach a firm conclusion) on the identity of Vuestra Merced: it is, he argues, the Archpriest himself. Darío Villanueva (*58*) examines the problem of the picaresque novels' addressees and implied readers. In his most recent article, Shipley (*110*) returns to the question of Lázaro's character, unconvinced by arguments such as those advanced by Woods (*118*) and soon to be advanced by Pamela Waley (*115*). Peter N. Dunn (*79*) considers what we should make of this narrative in the form of a confessional letter, and, finally, Vilanova (*114*: 180-236 and 280-325) looks more generally at Lazarillo's early training and at the adult Lázaro's position as autobiographer.

CHAPTER 8. The list of literary analogues and possible sources has been extended, and sources and traditions previously suggested have been further examined, by Francisco R. Adrados (*61*, the *Life of Aesop*), Dino S. Cervigni (*70*, Benvenuto Cellini's *Vita*), Dunn (*79*, confessional letters; cf. *75*: 81-103), Vilanova (*114*: 126-59, Apuleius), and Michael Zappala (*120*, Lucian). The folkloric side of *LT*'s literary ancestry has also been further explored, from different points of view: Angelo Morino's application of Bakhtin's concept of Carnival (*103*: 147-93), Maxime Chevalier's study of the way in which folktales cohere into a novel (*72*; cf. *87*: Chap. 3), Edmond Cros's study of various folkloric aspects (*75*: 5-20), Margit Frenk's application of the 'Law of Three' (*85*), and most recently Augustin Redondo's survey of Tratados 1-3 (*99*). It is a pity that one important study of *LT*'s context remains unpublished: John C. Dagenais, 'The Medieval Background of *LT* and the Picaresque' (doctoral thesis, University of Illinois, 1982).

CHAPTER 9. Most of the studies relevant to this chapter have been discussed above: Woods (*118*), Shipley (*107-08, 110*), and Waley (*115*). Two others must be mentioned: E.R. Davey (*77*) on the concept of man, looked at earlier, in a different way, by R.W. Truman (*41*); and John J. Allen (*63*), who sees more hope for individuals and society reflected in *LT* than in its picaresque successors.

In the light of these and other studies, I have of course modified my views on particular points discussed in this Guide, but they have not led me to abandon or radically change the main direction of my reading of *LT*. Indeed, most of the subsequent studies accept, explicitly or implicitly, that kind of reading. A partial exception is Paul Julian Smith (*112*: 98), who advocates a critical reading that 'does not linger in the narrative space [...] It is deflected back to ourselves.' Though some of what Smith says about *LT* is hard to reconcile with the way in which I read the text,[1] the words just quoted differ more in critical vocabulary than in substance from what I say in the Introduction and Conclusion to this Guide. I am surprised that Smith continues: 'But there is no direct "mirroring" of reader in the text. The story is not "about" us.' (A footnote attributes to me — 'As Deyermond claims [...]' — the view that Smith has rejected.) If I had said that the reader is directly mirrored in the text, Smith would be justified in his objection, but I said nothing of the kind; the first page of my Introduction makes it clear that my view is the opposite: I say that 'the relevance of literature is seldom direct' (p.9), and I devote almost a page to an explanation of what I mean. I return, on p.98, to what I mean by saying that 'The story, in short, is

---

[1]For instance: 'The story [...] reminds us in exemplary fashion of the provisional nature of all representation, of misrecognition as the absent origin from which all sense of self is derived' (*112*: 98).

about us'. As readers will easily be able to confirm, it is not what Smith alleges that I mean.

If I were to write this Guide afresh, there are aspects that I should wish to develop more adequately. One is the curious coincidence in a number of respects between Juan Rodríguez del Padrón's *Siervo libre de amor* (see p.11, n.3, below) and *LT*. For instance, the prefatory letter to *Siervo libre* refers to 'La muy agria relación del caso [que] por escriptura demandas saber', and cites Cicero.[2] It is highly unlikely that the author of *LT* read *Siervo libre*, which — unlike other sentimental romances — had not then been printed, and which survives in only one manuscript. We need, therefore, to look to a common tradition (see, as a starting-point, 60: 10, n.22). Secondly, I should wish to make use of studies in narratology published in recent years, looking more closely — among other topics — at narrative point of view.[3] Thirdly, I realize that my treatment of women and of female societies in *LT* is inadequate, and that a good deal of revision and amplification is needed; this will clearly need to take into account some of the findings of feminist criticism.[4] Fourthly, and for the moment finally, I should wish to integrate what I say in Chapter 2 about society with what I say in Chapter 3 about *LT* and religion (p.21, among others, makes a start with that integration). I now see how *LT* fits into the final phase of a book on which I have been intermittently working for the last few years: *The Social Gospel in Medieval Spanish Literature*. I mean by this the convergence of Christian teaching and Biblical allusion with social criticism, often of a radical kind. Such convergence is, of course, found in the Bible itself ('He hath put down the mighty from their seat, and hath exalted the humble and

---

[2]Juan Rodríguez del Padrón, *Obras completas*, ed. César Hernández Alonso (Madrid: Editora Nacional, 1982), p.155.

[3]Cf. my 'El punto de vista narrativo en la ficción sentimental del siglo XV', in *Actas del I Congreso de la Asociación Hispánica de Literatura Medieval, Santiago de Compostela, 2 al 6 de diciembre de 1985*, ed. Vicente Beltrán (Barcelona: PPU, 1988), pp.45-60.

[4]Cf. my 'Female Societies in *Celestina*', in *Fernando de Rojas and 'Celestina': Approaching the Fifth Centenary*, ed. Ivy A. Corfis & Joseph Snow (Madison: Hispanic Seminary of Medieval Studies, in press).

meek', says Mary in the Magnificat, Luke 1:52), but its working out
in Spanish literature has never been adequately studied.

All this, and more, would have its place in a Guide written in
1992, but for the present I hope that this Preface and the Supplementary Bibliography will suffice.[5]

Alan Deyermond
October 1992

Abbreviations

BHS	*Bulletin of Hispanic Studies*
HR	*Hispanic Review*
LNL	*Les Langues Néo-Latines*
LT	*Lazarillo de Tormes*
MLN	*Modern Language Notes*
MLR	*Modern Language Review*
NRFH	*Nueva Revista de Filología Hispánica*
PMLA	*Publications of the Modern Language Association*

---

[5]As explained in the Preface to the first edition, references to the text of
LT are to R.O. Jones's edition (*12*). Italic numerals refer to the
Bibliographical Note and Supplementary Bibliography. I am grateful to Dr
Catherine Davies for her comments on this Preface. She is not, of course,
responsible for any of the opinions that I have expressed. I repeat the
thanks expressed in the 1975 Preface to Dr Carole Adams, to the late
Professor P.R.K. Halkhoree, and to Professor J.E. Varey.

1 Introduction

De te fabula narratur – the story is about you. This favourite tag of medieval and Renaissance writers is as true today as it ever was. All great literature, and much that is not great, is about us. When a hero or a villain brings disaster or ridicule on himself or on others, the bell tolls for the reader. But, of course, the relevance of literature is seldom direct; rather, it works by analogy. Reading, we learn to apply to our own experience the stories of those who may, at first sight, have nothing in common with us; and the effort of comparison, the perception of the analogy, will enrich our experience and help us to understand facets of our lives and characters which had hitherto been comfortably hidden. In stripping off the layers of analogical covering from what we read, we are likely also to strip off the protective layers of self-deception from our own actions and motives. That is the primary moral function of literature, and it need not depend on the open assertion of a moral by the writer.

The analogical covering, the peel on the orange, differs greatly in thickness from one work to another. Contemporary novels and plays, written in English and realistic in tone, make less demand on our powers of imagination and perception than do works written centuries ago, or in another language, or about a different world. Don Quixote, Segismundo and Basilio, Racine's heroes and heroines, Julius Caesar and Mark Antony, Sauron and Gandalf, resemble us less obviously (though perhaps not less strongly) than Oliver Twist, Billy Liar, or even the characters of *La colmena*. Of course, a book whose relevance was immediately apparent to its first readers may, by the passage of time or shifts in literary fashion, become unfamiliar to later readers, as has happened with the picaresque novels of Spain's Golden Age. There is insufficient space here for a discussion of the nature and origins of the genre, and good, sometimes excellent, treatments of this question already exist.[1] It is enough to say that, at least in sixteenth and seventeenth-

[1] In addition to the works listed in section C of the Bibliographical Note, see the

century Spain, picaresque novels are to some extent episodic in
construction, almost always narrated in the first person, and well
supplied with comic incident; the setting is low life, and the atmos-
phere that of delinquency;[2] and the novels point a moral, either
directly (as in *Guzmán de Alfarache*, 1599 and 1604) or by
implication (as in *Lazarillo de Tormes*).

Lazarillo is the story of a boy of poor and disreputable parentage
who, at a tender age, is placed in service with a blind man; whose
deceits and misadventures while with this master and with this
second, a priest, are recounted in detail; and who then serves a
squire so poor that Lazarillo's hunger is at first far worse than in
the previous episodes – so poor and shiftless, indeed, that Lazarillo
has to find food for them both. From these three masters, he learns
unedifying lessons: in particular, that of hypocrisy. These lessons
are reinforced by the subsequent episodes, all but one very sketchily
narrated, and are put fully into practice in Lázaro's young man-
hood, when he attains what he regards as a desirable and prosperous post, that of town crier of Toledo, and becomes the com-
plaisant husband of the Archpriest's mistress. All of this is told in
the first person, allegedly in response to a request from the Archpriest's friend that "se le escriba y relate el caso muy por extenso"
(*Pr.* 34–5).

Lazarillo's relation to the picaresque genre is a matter of dis-
pute: critical opinions range from Parker's statement that it is a
precursor, rather than a prototype (*4*, p. 6; cf. *12*, p. xxxix), to Guillén's view that it "remains, after five hundred years, the masterpiece of the genre" (*2*, p. 93). Most critics, however, accept *Lazarillo* as a picaresque novel, and rightly so. It has the features mentioned earlier, and its kinship with *Guzmán de Alfarache* was
recognized as soon as the latter work appeared (see *2*, pp. 72–3 and
135–58). It is true that almost half a century elapsed between the
first extant editions of *Lazarillo* and the publication of *Guzmán*,
and that for most of that time the evidence for *Lazarillo*'s popularity is patchy, but such a gap between a first, experimental work
and the main flowering of a genre occurs elsewhere.[3] It is also true

---

first chapter of Jennifer Lowe's Critical Guide, *Cervantes: Two novelas ejemplares*.

[2] Parker points out that the traditional term "roguery" now gives a misleading
impression, and that "delinquency" is more appropriate (*4*, pp. 3–6).

that the word *pícaro* does not occur in *Lazarillo*, and that the author shows no awareness of a picaresque tradition, but the use of the word is unimportant in comparison with the presentation of the character, and the founder of a tradition can hardly be expected to foresee the consequences of his work. What matters is that later picaresque writers were aware of their relationship, as is shown by the frontispiece to *La pícara Justina* (1605), which depicts Lazarillo rowing a boat which contains the bull of Salamanca, and towing "La nave de la vida pícara"; in the ship are Guzmán, Celestina and Justina (the frontispiece is reproduced in *4*, facing p. xii). It is sometimes said (e.g. by Parker, *4*, p. 144) that this dissociates *Lazarillo* from the genre, but I think it more likely that the artist's intention was to represent vividly the genre's dependence on this novel; the idea of a rowing boat may well have been suggested to him by the brevity of *Lazarillo* in comparison with other picaresque novels, and by the unusual variant, found at the end of the prologue, of the image of life as a sea voyage: "los que . . ., con fuerza y maña *remando*, salieron a buen puerto" (*Pr.* 39–40; my italics).

Three editions of *Lazarillo*, the first to survive, were published in 1554, at Burgos, Antwerp and Alcalá de Henares.[4] In all probability the Antwerp and Alcalá editions derive from one lost edition, and that in turn seems, together with the Burgos edition, to derive from a lost archetype or original edition, probably printed not more than a year or two before the first surviving ones.[5] None of the 1554 editions is wholly reliable, but apart from the Alcalá interpolations (see below), the differences are relatively minor. Recent editors have differed in their preferences: Guillén

---

[3] There is an exact parallel in pre-*Lazarillo* Spain: Juan Rodríguez del Padrón's *Estoria de dos amadores* (inset in his *Siervo libre de amor*, circa 1440) is the first Spanish sentimental romance, but the genre did not become firmly established until the 1490s, when the romances of Diego de San Pedro and Juan de Flores were published.

[4] All three are reproduced in facsimile in a single volume, with a brief introductory note by Enrique Moreno Báez (Cieza: la fonte que mana y corre, 1959).

[5] The bibliographical problems have long been discussed by scholars, were partially resolved by Cavaliere (*8*) and Caso González (*7*), and seem to have been finally settled by Rico, "En torno al texto crítico" (see *7*), and Blecua (*6*). Blecua has shown (pp. 52–6) that, despite the opinions of Jones (*12*, p. xvi) and Caso González, the extant editions derive not from manuscripts but from printed texts.

(*10*) bases his text on Antwerp, Caso González (*7*) on a combination of Antwerp and Alcalá, and Cavaliere (*8*), Riquer (*14*), Jones (*12*), Rico (*13*) and Blecua (*6*) on Burgos. The best text can probably be obtained by applying the established methods of textual criticism to correct Burgos when it seems to diverge from the lost archetype; this is Blecua's method.

The Alcalá edition contains six passages absent from Burgos and Antwerp: a substantial episode is added to *Tratado* I and another to *Tratado* V, and four brief passages are interpolated (one in V, and three in VII). These interpolations are differently treated by modern editors: Cavaliere and Jones print them in an appendix, Rico in footnotes, and Caso González combines the two methods; Riquer and Blecua incorporate them into the text in italics, and Guillén omits them entirely. Both the Riquer-Blecua method and that of Guillén are regrettable, since the first makes the interpolations seem part of the authentic text (like Fernando de Rojas's interpolations in *La Celestina*), and the second implies that they are unimportant. They are in fact of considerable interest, since although there is no reason to think that they are by the original author, they are the earliest evidence that we have of his contemporaries' attitude to the novel, and show a keen insight into his methods. Several of them strengthen the structural devices used by the author, especially that of prophecy and fulfilment, and though they are more obvious than the author would have made them, these passages provide unmistakable support for the modern critical emphasis on the novel's unity. The last of the interpolations, "de lo que de aquí adelante me sucediere avisaré a vuestra merced", leaves the way open for a sequel, and one duly appeared (Antwerp, 1555). Thereafter, interest in *Lazarillo de Tormes* seems to have decreased, reviving when *Guzmán de Alfarache* appeared.[6]

The author frames the beginning and end of his novel in references to two historical events: Lazarillo's father dies in "cierta armada contra moros . . ., la de los Gelves" (1. 15 and 72–3), and Lázaro refuses to listen to gossip about his wife in "el mesmo año

---

[6] It is difficult to measure this decrease by the number of editions between 1555 and 1599, because the disapproval of the Inquisition reduced their number. For an outline history of early editions and references, see *12*, pp. xxxix–xlii; *35*, pp. 95–141 (Rico challenges the general assumption that there was a substantial decline in interest); and *6*, pp. 46–8.

que nuestro victorioso Emperador en esta insigne ciudad de Toledo
entró y tuvo en ella cortes" (7. 77–8). On this basis, attempts have
been made to date the composition of the book, but in vain: there
were two expeditions to Los Gelves (1510 and 1520), and two
Cortes (1525 and 1538); if that difficulty were removed, we should
have an earliest possible date for composition, but the novel could
have been written at any time between that date (i.e. 1525 or 1538)
and 1553, since it need not have been written in the year in which,
according to Lázaro, the action ends. Certainty is, then, unattain-
able, but some deductions may be made from other types of evidence. When works circulate in manuscript for a long time before
they are published, it is often possible to find references to them, yet
there seem to be no pre-1554 references to *Lazarillo*. Composition
in the early 1550s would fit the pattern of documentary references
to social problems similar to those found in *Lazarillo*, and would
also coincide with a flowering of autobiographical and pseudo-
autobiographical literature (*16*, p. 50; *26*, pp. 13–57).[7]

Finally, there is the problem of the work's anonymity. An occasional eccentric critic has taken seriously the claim that the author
was town crier of Toledo, but there is near-universal agreement
that only a man of considerable culture could have produced this
complex, economical and allusive book. A detailed discussion of
the question would be outside the scope of this Critical Guide, and
in any case I have no new contribution to make. However, it may
be useful to indicate briefly which candidates for authorship have
been suggested. For some sixty years after the publication of
Lazarillo, no names seem to have been mentioned, so we lack
evidence from the author's contemporaries, but two were suggested
in the early seventeenth century, when, as Jones points out, oral
tradition about the novel's composition may still have been circulat-
ing. One is Juan de Ortega, who became General of the Hieronymite Order in 1552, and the other is the poet and historian Diego
Hurtado de Mendoza. What we know of each of these men is consistent with his having written the novel, and there is some positive

[7] Most recent editors, and authors of longer studies, have discussed the date of
composition. Blecua (*6*, pp. 9–15) has a most useful summary of the discussion,
with his own persuasive arguments for late composition. See also Natale Rossi,
"Sulla datazione del *LT*", in *Studi di Letteratura Spagnola* (Roma: Società
Filologica Romana, 1966 [1968]), pp. 169–80.

evidence in support of each. Ortega is perhaps the stronger candidate, if only because he was not known as a writer; there would thus be little reason to attribute *Lazarillo* to him unless there was a strong tradition within his Order that he had written it (the attribution was made by a fellow Hieronymite, Juan de Sigüenza, the historian of the Order). All the other candidates are much later suggestions: the poet, dramatist and proverb-collector Sebastián de Horozco; the dramatist Lope de Rueda; and the humanists Juan de Valdés, Hernán Núñez, and Pedro de Rúa. There is nothing inherently unlikely about any of these except for Lope de Rueda, but on the other hand there is not much positive evidence, and none is as likely as Ortega or Mendoza. It seems increasingly probable that we shall never know either the identity of the author or his reason for anonymity.[8]

---

[8] For recent and judicious summaries of the authorship controversy, see *12*, pp. ix–xii; *13*, pp. xvi–xxv; *21*, pp. 19–35; and *6*, pp. 44–6.

Lazarillo de Tormes offers its readers a picture of Spanish society in the first half of the sixteenth century; a picture that is vivid, amusing, and unpleasant. Is it also realistic? Until recently, English-speaking readers at least were in no doubt. The first British translator, David Rowland, assured his patron that "besides much mirth, here is also a true discription of the nature and disposition of sundrie Spaniards. So that by reading hereof, such as have not travailed Spaine, may as well discerne much of the maners and customs of that countrey, as those that have there long time continued."[1] The same view was taken by a friend of Rowland's who contributed a poem to close the volume:

> Then Lazaro deserves
>   no blame, but praise to gaine,
> That plainly pens the Spaniards pranks
>   and how they live in Spaine.   (p. 75)

Two and a half centuries later, we find in H. J. Chaytor's introduction to his once influential edition of *Lazarillo* the same conviction that this is a realistic picture, and the same note of moral disapprobation: "the towns were filled with idlers who had forgotten the arts of peace and the habit of steady industry . . . here again is a picture of Spain in her early decadence, using every shift to maintain a brave front and desperately clinging to her faded tinsel with a pride that nothing can abate" (Manchester: University Press, 1922, pp. xiv–xvi). This will not do: there is, as we shall see, a good deal in the book that reflects social reality, but to regard it as a primarily realistic picture is to fall into a double error. First, it is wrong to assume that an unpleasant description is necessarily more realistic than an idealized one; they may well, especially in medi-

---

[1] *The Pleasaunt Historie of Lazarillo de Tormes, drawen out of Spanish by David Rouland of Anglesey, 1586*, ed. J. E. V. Crofts (The Percy Reprints, VII, Oxford: Blackwell, 1924), p. 3. See Dale B. J. Randall, *The Golden Tapestry: a critical survey of non-chivalric Spanish fiction in English translation (1543–1657)* (Durham, N. C.: Duke Univ. Press, 1963), pp. 57–66.

eval and Renaissance literature, be equally distant from reality, and
be the result of a technique of selective exaggeration. Secondly,
Spain's economic and political decline was half a century away in
the future when *Lazarillo* was published; as Lomax shows, the
first half of the sixteenth century was an age of economic boom
and political expansion (*28*, p. 375). There were clouds in the sky –
rural poverty and recurring local famines were endemic, as in any
country at that time (*28*, pp. 373–4), the benefits of economic expansion were unevenly spread, and there was the occasional
politico-military setback – but it is hard to agree with Del Monte
that the Spain of Charles V was economically exhausted and milit-
arily unsuccessful, and that *Lazarillo* is "una fábula amarga e
irónica nacida del pesimismo y que simbolizaba en las aventuras de
un muchacho las aventuras de la España de su tiempo, olvidadiza
de su idealidad de la Reconquista, tarada por la miseria y pagada
de un esplendor vano y caduco" (*1*, p. 40).

Nevertheless, society is presented to us in this novel as corrupt,
hypocritical, impoverished, and corrupting (whether this is the
author's view, or merely that of the mature Lázaro who tells the
story, is a matter for individual judgment). Corrupt: theft and
fraud (on the latter, see *17*) are prevalent, and the ministers of
justice and of the church are as deeply involved in them as anyone
else. Sexual corruption receives less emphasis, but even if we dis-
count the liaison of Lázaro's mother and the birth of his bastard
half-brother in *Tratado* I (though contemporary readers might not
have discounted this), we are given the strongest of hints that the
clergy take advantage of their status to indulge their lusts, whether
homosexual (the Mercedarian Friar, 4. 8–9) or adulterous (the
Archpriest of San Salvador, *Tratado* VII). Most serious of all, the
clergy and the gentry are shown as betraying their essential functions: the Priest of Maqueda, the Friar and the Archpriest show
no concern for the spiritual welfare of their flocks; the Squire
dreams of becoming a perfidious adviser to a great lord (3. 514–30),
he is unable to maintain or protect his servant, he can eat only because the neighbours take pity on Lazarillo, and, faced with a
crisis, he runs away. We are a long way from what was still the pre-
vailing social theory of the Three Estates, in which the function of
each estate complemented those of the others, so that knights

(squires were included) protected not only themselves but the whole of society, the clergy looked after the spiritual and intellectual life of society, and all were fed by the labours of the peasants.[2] In place of this mutual help and specialization of function, there is naked, and not even very successful, self-interest. Neither is there much encouragement, in Lazarillo's society, to behave differently. The Constable of *Tratado* VII tries to do his duty:

> una noche nos corrieron a mí y a mi amo a pedradas y a palos unos retraídos, y a mi amo, que esperó, trataron mal, mas a mí no me alcanzaron.   (7. 3–5)

Hypocritical: not one of Lazarillo's masters in *Tratados* I–V is what he seems or what he claims. The Blind Man's piety and benevolence are a sham, the Priest's hypocrisy is extreme and all-pervading, the Squire's fastidious insistence on honour is in shameful and ludicrous conflict with the facts of his existence, the Friar is "gran enemigo del coro . . ., amicísimo de negocios seglares" (4. 3–5), the Pardoner is a canting trickster. Only the two masters in *Tratado* VI, and the Constable in *Tratado* VII, seem free from hypocrisy, but they are mentioned so briefly that they make little impression (and should a Chaplain be in the water-selling trade?). In any case, the pattern of a society riddled with hypocrisy is now firmly fixed in the reader's mind, it will be reinforced by the behaviour of the Archpriest in the second part of *Tratado* VII, and, perhaps most important of all, Lázaro has by now learned the lesson his masters taught him by example, and has become an accomplished hypocrite: he runs away as soon as the Constable is in danger (7. 3–5), and when confronted with what he must know to be well-founded gossip about his wife, he replies: "yo juraré sobre la hostia consagrada que es tan buena mujer como vive dentro de las puertas de Toledo" (7. 73–4). By a further irony, the squalid and degraded Blind Man, whom the Priest, the Squire and

---

[2] "Todos los estados del mundo . . . se ençierran en tres: al uno llaman defensores, et al otro oradores, et al otro labradores" (Juan Manuel, *Libro de los estados*, Chap. XCII). This medieval theory persisted well into the sixteenth century. Some critics have suggested that *Tratados* I–III represent the three estates, but this is implausible: the Blind Man cannot be taken as a representative of *labradores*. However, the juxtaposition of Priest and Squire can hardly be accidental.

the others would have despised, is closer than those others to being what he seems. It would be overstating the case a little to say that he has his own kind of repulsive integrity, but he is certainly less unctuously hypocritical than his social superiors. The hypocrisy, the moral quicksands, of Lazarillo's world have a stylistic equivalent in the transformation of objects into something unexpected (see pp. 55–6, below).

Impoverished: the theme of hunger, insistent throughout the first three *Tratados* and reaching a climax in the third, is the most obvious manifestation, but it is reinforced by the small scale of Lázaro's successes (not only the final and precarious success of *Tratado* VII, but the four years' good earnings and assiduous saving needed to acquire shabby second-hand clothes, 6. 13–15), and the pitifully small amounts of food and money for which Lazarillo and his masters contend so hard. The contrast between extreme effort and diminutive reward is, of course, for comic effect, but it also paints a picture of a society in which poverty is habitual and desperation normal.

Corrupting: the adult Lázaro's narrative lays on society the blame for what he has become. The Blind Man taught the boy, by precept and by example, to be dishonest and cynical, the Priest and the Pardoner reinforced the lesson, the Squire showed him how little contact there was between real and apparent honour, and showed him also the consequences of feeling pity for a fellow mortal, and the Friar made it clear that those in authority could indulge their sexual appetites with impunity. Even if, as some critics say, we should treat Lázaro's account with suspicion, the fact remains that society is here presented to us as a corrupting force.

To a considerable extent, this gloomy vision of society is traditional. Corruption, hypocrisy and betrayal of function are the targets of preachers and satirists throughout the closing centuries of the Middle Ages. Examples abound, in Spain and elsewhere: in the thirteenth century the debate poem *Elena y María* shows us a lustful and hypocritical priest, and a knight so impoverished by gambling that he has to pawn his mistress's clothes and his own armour; at the end of the fourteenth century Pero López de Ayala, in the *Rimado de palacio*, surveys the different groups of

Castilian society and finds them all to blame; in the fifteenth century the anonymous satirical poems, *Coplas de ¡Ay panadera!*, *Coplas del Provincial* and *Coplas de Mingo Revulgo*, use different techniques – including humour, sexual scandal and revolting physical detail – for a common purpose, the exposure of hypocrisy and corruption, and the denunciation of society as a whole.[3] It is unnecessary to suppose that any of these poems is a specific source of *Lazarillo*; there is a continuing tradition, and *Lazarillo* is clearly part of it. Another aspect of the tradition is found in sermons: not enough is yet known about the medieval Spanish popular sermon, but its English counterpart shows that preachers were as aware as poets of social failings, and as eager to use against them any weapons that came to hand.[4]

The traditional nature of *Lazarillo*'s gloom about society does not, however, mean that it has no basis in the social reality of the mid-sixteenth century. The documents of the Cortes for this period (see *32*) show concern with such problems as beggars from other towns (1518), wandering orphans and deserted children (1548), the misbehaviour of pardoners (1512), and the growing number of unemployable and impoverished *hidalgos* (1528). Other types of evidence confirm the picture (*6*, pp. 16–20). Even some apparently exaggerated details may reflect the reality of the times more closely than one would expect. The simulated fit of the Pardoner's accomplice in church may seem merely fantastic:

> el negro alguacil cae de su estado y da tan gran golpe en el suelo que la iglesia toda hizo resonar, y comenzó a bramar y echar espumajos por la boca y torcella, y hacer visajes con el gesto, dando de pie y de mano, revolviéndose por aquel suelo a una parte y a otra.   (5. 104–8)

A close parallel is, however, to be found in the life of Juan de Dios (1495–1550), who was converted on hearing San Juan de Ávila preach in Granada:

---

[3] These poems, or the relevant extracts from them, are all to be found in Julio Rodríguez-Puértolas, *Poesía de protesta en la Edad Media castellana: historia y antología* (Madrid: Gredos, 1968), as are other works which could equally well be cited, such as the *Danza de la Muerte*.

[4] G. R. Owst, *Literature and Pulpit in Medieval England: a neglected chapter in the history of English letters and of the English people* (2nd ed., Oxford: Blackwell, 1961), Ch. V–VII.

Se arrojava por el suelo, dándose cabeçadas por las paredes, y
arrancándose las barvas y las cejas, y haziendo otras cosas, que
fácilmente sospecharon todos que avía perdido el juyzio.[5]

On the one hand, then, we have a satirical tradition; on the
other, frequent similarities between life as presented in *Lazarillo*
and the evidence of contemporary documents. Fortunately, there
is no real conflict: preachers and poets consistently attacked corruption, hypocrisy, the keeping of mistresses by priests, and other
social ills precisely because they were social ills which obstinately
recurred. Yet we should not assume that because the background
of *Lazarillo* corresponds to real life, all the incidents can be similarly documented. Most of the main incidents, especially in the early
Tratados, derive not from reality but from folklore and literature
(see Ch. 8, below). This brings us back to the point made at the
beginning of this chapter: the overall impression of Spanish
society given in the novel does not correspond to reality, since we
are shown only the black parts of the picture.

The emphasis on corruption and hypocrisy is, as we have seen,
traditional. This is to be expected: a writer who wants to attack
abuses – and it is clear that, despite the manifold ambiguities of
Lazarillo, this is one of the writer's aims – will inevitably concen-
trate on what is wrong with society. As to the emphasis on poverty,
this is not too hard to reconcile with the general prosperity of the
period, since, as we have seen, that prosperity coexisted with social
and geographical pockets of deprivation. These had always existed,
and the breakdown of the European feudal system (and of the
approximation to it which was found in Spain) made things worse
for many people though better for others. Lomax rightly points out
that, in a period of increasing general prosperity, local poverty and
famine is more noticeable (*28*, p. 376). His view of *Lazarillo* as
part of a "revolution of rising expectations" reinforces Jones's
opinion that "the book is probably in part a protest against the
wretched lot of the poor in sixteenth-century Spain" (*12*, p. xxvi;
cf. *27*, p. 351). This does not exclude humour: we are dealing

5 Francisco de Castro, *Historia de la vida y sanctas obras de Juan de Dios*
(Granada, 1585). I owe this quotation to P. E. Russell, "The *Celestina comentada*",
in *Medieval Hispanic Studies Presented to Rita Hamilton* (London: Tamesis,
1975, p. 179); I have slightly regularized the spelling and have supplied accents.

with a period when misfortune and suffering were thought comic (in Western Europe as recently as the eighteenth century physical deformity provoked jeers, and a visit to a lunatic asylum was an agreeable diversion), but we must remember other aspects of the traditions of the time. The Biblical connotations of the name Lázaro, with the condemnation of the rich man who was indifferent to Lazarus's suffering, would in themselves justify the interpretation of this novel as, among other things, a social protest. And those connotations do not stand alone. One of the Seven Corporal Works of Mercy, imposed as a duty by the Catholic Church, was the relief of poverty, and the failure of the more prosperous characters in the novel to carry out that duty (unless, as in the Archpriest's case, it is for an ulterior motive) is blatant. It links the emphasis on poverty to the picture of a corrupt and selfish society.

3 *"Lazarillo de Tormes" and religion*

We have seen that the Church plays a large part in the corrupt society of this novel. It also exercises a profound influence on Lazarillo's life: three of his masters are clerics, a fourth (the Pardoner) operates on the fringes of the clergy, and his patron and cuckolder in *Tratado* VII is the Archpriest. As Del Monte says, "la vida de Lázaro casi se desarrolla bajo la protección de la Iglesia" (*1*, p. 45); what is more, the influence is, with one possible exception, evil. This destructive portrait of the clergy need not imply hostility to Christianity, or even to the Catholic Church: for centuries devout Christians, including high-ranking clerics, had denounced and satirized abuses in the priesthood and the administration of the Church. Some of Lázaro's comments, and some words of other characters, go further, since they imply that ecclesiastical corruption and self-interest are the norm, not the exception:

> No nos maravillemos de un clérigo ni fraile, porque el uno hurta de los pobres y el otro de casa para sus devotas y para ayuda de otro tanto, cuando a un pobre esclavo el amor le animaba a esto. (1. 50–4)
> No sé si de su cosecha era [la avaricia], o lo había anexado con el hábito de clerecía. (2. 10–12)[1]

and the Priest's "Toma, come, triunfa, que para ti es el mundo. Mejor vida tienes que el Papa" (2. 42–3). These sentences make it clear that the author was, at the least, hostile to the existing state of the Church, and of course they raise the possibility that he felt a more general scepticism about Christian belief itself. Is there anything in the text which might turn that possibility into a probability?

First, the protagonist's attitude to God reveals a variety of Christian belief that is self-centred and shallow to an extreme. The earliest references to God in the novel are orthodox enough: for

---

[1] These two sentences of generalized comment, together with the whole of *Tratados* IV and V, are suppressed in the expurgated edition of 1573 (6, p. 37).

example, Lázaro mentions "Mi padre, que Dios perdone" (1.5). Some of these have an ironic twist, but there is nothing to make one suspect a fundamentally subversive attitude to religion. Soon, however, Lázaro's words make it clear that for him God is equated with good luck, arranging matters so that he may gain food, money or revenge, irrespective of the suffering of others.[2] For example:

> Dios le cegó aquella hora el entendimiento (fue por darme dél venganza).   (1. 402–3)
> Y porque dije de mortuorios, Dios me perdone, que jamás fui enemigo de la naturaleza humana sino entonces, y esto era porque comíamos bien y me hartaban. Deseaba y aun rogaba a Dios que cada día matase el suyo.   (2. 68–72)
> Vino el mísero de mi amo, y quiso Dios no miró en la oblada que el ángel había llevado.   (2. 126–8)
> Andando así discurriendo de puerta en puerta, con harto poco remedio, porque ya la caridad se subió al cielo, topóme Dios con un escudero que iba por la calle con razonable vestido, bien peinado, su paso y compás en orden.   (3. 11–14)
> Y pensando en qué modo de vivir haría mi asiento por tener descanso y ganar algo para la vejez, quiso Dios alumbrarme y ponerme en camino y manera provechosa.   (7. 7–9)[3]

References of this type are, perhaps significantly, most heavily concentrated in *Tratado* II, in which Lazarillo's adversary is the Priest. It is certainly possible to read into them a strong hint by the author that God is no more than a name that we give to our luck, that Lázaro's attitude is representative of all men's, and that the whole of Christian doctrine is mere decoration covering this central and selfish fiction. Such a reading would, however, almost certainly be mistaken. The mature Lázaro, whose attitude is embodied in the words quoted above, is presented for our disapproval (even if also for our recognition of some uncomfortably close resemblances to ourselves), and his attitude to God is of a piece with his hypocrisy, his self-indulgence and his other vices. There is nothing in the text to suggest that the author endorses his attitude.

---

[2] See *19*, pp. 251–4, for parallels in other works; other sections of this article contain additional information on the protagonist's religious attitude.
[3] See Gilman's comments on such sentences (*22*, pp. 156–7).

Secondly, there is the question of parody. A number of passages, especially in the first two *tratados*, are Biblical quotations or reminiscences, and almost without exception they are placed in unsuitable contexts. Lazarillo's father is referred to in terms which the Bible applies to John the Baptist, and a passage from the Sermon on the Mount is twisted to provide a pseudo-justification for his thefts (see pp. 47–8 and 53, below). Lazarillo's awakening to the deceitfulness of the world – "Parecióme que en aquel instante desperté de la simpleza en que como niño dormido estaba" (1. 97–8) – is a probably deliberate echo of St Paul's "When I was a child, I spake as a child, I understood as a child, I thought as a child : but when I became a man, I put away childish things" (I Corinthians xiii. 11). If Lazarillo's awakening had led to a rejection of the world, the strictest Christian orthodoxy would have been satisfied, but instead it makes him determined to win the world's game by its own rules: "me cumple avivar el ojo y avisar, pues solo soy, y pensar cómo me sepa valer" (1. 99–100) – the opposite, in fact, of Paul's conclusion that "now abideth faith, hope, charity, these three; but the greatest of these is charity". Even more startling is the implicit equation of the Blind Man with St Peter and then with Christ: "Yo oro ni plata no te lo puedo dar, mas avisos para vivir muchos te mostraré" (1. 104–5; cf. "Silver and gold have I none, but such as I have give I thee: In the name of Jesus Christ of Nazareth rise up and walk", Acts iii. 6), which is followed by "después de Dios éste me dio la vida, y siendo ciego me alumbró y adestró en la carrera de vivir" (1. 106–7; cf. "Jesus saith unto him, I am the way, the truth, and the life: no man cometh unto the Father, but by me", John xiv. 6). And there are other examples.[4] The effect of these passages is reinforced by the Pardoner's adaptation of standard prayers from the liturgy (5. 86–7 and 156–7), and by the emphasis in *Tratado* I on wine and in *Tratado* II on bread : this juxtaposition strengthens the eucharistic symbolism which

[4] Cf. 2. 352–3 with Matthew xii. 40 (discussed at the end of this chapter); 3. 194–5 with Deuteronomy xxxii. 39 and Job v. 17–18; and 3. 199–200 with Romans xi. 33. With the exception of 1. 106–7 (pointed out by Perry, *33*, pp. 143–4) and of 1.97–8, all of these passages of Biblical origin are noted by recent editors. Truman (*40*, p. 604) suggests other possible Biblical parodies, including an alternative origin for 1. 106–7, though this is less satisfactory than Perry's.

would in any case be evoked by such words as "abro el arca, y como vi el pan, comencélo de adorar, no osando recebillo" (2. 151–2).

The use of Biblical and liturgical allusions in such scandalously inappropriate contexts might today seem incompatible with Christian belief on the author's part, but when this novel was written, there was a centuries-old tradition of accommodating sacred texts to profane contexts, as entertaining parody, or as satire directed at abuses in the Church, or of course for a combination of these reasons. The parodies in *Lazarillo de Tormes* are designed to amuse, and most of them are also intended to emphasize the corruption of society and the growing corruption of Lazarillo. There is, then, no reason to conclude that the author's obvious scepticism about some aspects of the Church extended to Christianity itself. It is admittedly not possible to prove that the author was a convinced Christian, although the use made of the two Lazarus figures of the New Testament (discussed later in this chapter) suggests rather strongly that he was. In any case, atheistic and agnostic views, though certainly to be found in mid-sixteenth-century Spain, were uncommon, and we should need strong evidence before deciding that they were held by the author of this novel (see 35, pp. 52–5).

Such a theory has not been seriously advanced, but two types of deviation from the Spanish Catholic tradition have been suggested. Some scholars believe that the author was an Erasmian, a member of a reforming group within the Catholic Church which preferred personal devotion to outward ritual, and which encouraged study of the Bible and the participation of the laity in areas previously reserved for the clergy.[5] This seems on balance to be unlikely, chiefly because the book's anticlericalism is of a medieval rather than an Erasmian type, attacking avarice and sexual immorality rather than shortcomings in belief, and also because of the author's fondness for Biblical parody (see 26, pp. 184–5). The conclusion reached by Marcel Bataillon, the greatest authority on the Spanish Erasmians, seems to be correct: "Aunque la novelita respira el aire de una época dominada por Erasmo, no respira el del eras-

[5] The fundamental study is Marcel Bataillon's *Erasmo y España*, trans. Antonio Alatorre (2nd ed., México: Fondo de Cultura Económica, 1966).

mismo militante" (*16*, p. 17).[6] The same verdict should probably be given, with even greater emphasis, on suggestions that the author was an *alumbrado*, or member of the Illuminist movement, which stressed individual religious experience, and which was influenced by the Erasmians.[7]

A more widely held view is that the author was a *converso* – that is, that he came from a Jewish family which had been converted to Christianity. Most conversions were made in the fifteenth century, usually under pressure (the wish to escape persecution by the mob, or, at the end of the century, exile by the government). There was consequently a good deal of doubt as to the sincerity of the conversions, even after several generations. In some cases the doubt was well founded (some families continued to practise Judaism in secret), while in others Christian belief was genuine; but it was difficult to distinguish the one from the other, and that difficulty was the reason, or the pretext, for the Inquisition's hounding of many *conversos*. The suspicion and fear engendered by this situation had increasingly harmful effects on Spanish society in the sixteenth century,[8] and since *conversos* were prominent in literature and intellectual life generally, one would expect their problems to be reflected in a fair number of literary works. Here again, there is a difficulty : it is not always possible to determine whether an author is of Jewish ancestry; it is seldom possible to know whether a proven *converso* was a sincere Christian, a secret adherent of Judaism, or an agnostic; and there is no agreement on typically *converso* features of literary works. It is unlikely, for the reasons given above, that the author of *Lazarillo* was fundamental-

[6] For the contrary view, see Manuel J. Asensio, "La intención religiosa del *LT* y Juan de Valdés", *HR*, XXVII (1959), 78–102; Francisco Márquez Villanueva, "La actitud espiritual del *LT*", in *Espiritualidad y literatura en el siglo XVI* (Madrid : Alfaguara, 1968), pp. 67–137; Rico, *13*, pp. lviii–lxii; and Parker, *4*, p. 24. For a possible trace of Erasmian influence which is consistent with Bataillon's opinion, see Concha, *19*, pp. 258–9; Concha later, p. 272, confirms Bataillon's conclusion.

[7] Asensio, "La intención religiosa", suggests, in addition to his main theory of Erasmian authorship, that the author may have been an *alumbrado* of *converso* origin (see the next paragraph).

[8] See Stephen Gilman, *The Spain of Fernando de Rojas: the intellectual and social landscape of La Celestina* (Princeton : Univ. Press, 1972). Although some aspects of this book have been justifiably criticized, it offers a vivid, and in general convincing, reconstruction of the problems facing *conversos* in the first half of the century.

ly hostile to Christianity, but it is entirely possible that he was a
converso. Those who have seen evidence of a *converso* background
in the book include Castro (*11*), Guillén (*10*, p. 33), Gilman (*22*),
Lázaro Carreter (*26*, p. 185), and Rico (*34*, p. 290), though they
feel different degrees of conviction, and some of their views need
to be re-examined in the light of Concha's detailed and well-
documented objections (*19*). The complexity of the subject is
illustrated by the fact that, whereas some critics see the portrait of
the Squire – compared to a "galgo de buena casta", and ludicrously
obsessed with cleanliness – as a satire by a *converso* author against
the *cristianos viejos* and their preoccupation with "limpieza de
sangre", McGrady believes that the author is a *cristiano viejo*
aristocrat and the Squire a satirical portrait of a *converso* (*29*). And
there, in default of any firm evidence, the matter must be left.

There is another, and very important, side to the use of religious
material in *Lazarillo de Tormes*: its symbolic and structural value
in relation to the theme of the novel. The religious symbolism has
sometimes been exaggerated,[9] and this is unfortunately true of
Perry's study, which begins promisingly: his interpretation of the
Blind Man as the Devil and of Lazarillo as Adam tempted and
then cast out of Paradise (*33*, pp. 142–5; cf. *17*, pp. 51–2) seems to
strain the evidence unduly. Nevertheless, some such symbolism is
present: for example, the Priest's bread locked away in a chest, and
Lazarillo's attitude to it, evoke the Mass, as we have seen. The
novel's structure also seems to be affected by the religious background of the time; in this case, by the two ways in which the Old
Testament was seen to prepare the way for the New: prophecy
and its fulfilment, and typology or prefiguration (see pp. 37–8,
below).

The most important Biblical influence, however, is that embodied in the protagonist's name.[10] Bataillon (*16*, pp. 28–9) believes

[9] Anson C. Piper, "The 'Breadly Paradise' of *LT*", *Hispania* (U.S.A.), XLIV
(1961), 269–71; Jack Weiner, "La lucha de Lazarillo de Tormes por el arca", in
Actas del III Congreso Internacional de Hispanistas (México: Colegio de México,
1970), pp. 931–4. It is interesting that, although Miller does not mention Lazarillo's
"paraíso panal", he finds that "almost every picaresque novel has a *vision of
paradise* in it", and that these visions "contrast with the otherwise universal
chaos" (*3*, p. 97).

[10] Most of the remainder of this chapter comes from my article, "Lazarus and
Lazarillo", *Studies in Short Fiction*, II (1964–5), 351–7.

that the name of Lazarillo, and perhaps even of Lazarillo de
Tormes, was attached to precisely this kind of character in popular
tales which inspired our author. Most critics disagree with him,
preferring the view that the boy who plays tricks on his blind
master, and Lázaro as a name for a suffering man, are separate
traditions which are united for the first time in this novel. There
is general and long-standing agreement that the protagonist's name
was chosen because Lazarus is the Biblical prototype of a miserable
and suffering existence (9, pp. 13–16; *11*, p. vii; *14*, p. 89; and
many subsequent critics).[11] Lazarus the poor man is described
thus:

> There was a certain rich man, which was clothed in purple and
> fine linen, and fared sumptuously every day: And there was a
> certain beggar named Lazarus, which was laid at his gate, full
> of sores. And desiring to be fed with the crumbs which fell from
> the rich man's table: moreover the dogs came and licked his
> sores. And it came to pass, that the beggar died, and was carried
> by the angels into Abraham's bosom: the rich man also died,
> and was buried; And in hell he lift up his eyes, being in tor-
> ments, and seeth Abraham afar off, and Lazarus in his bosom.
> (Luke xvi. 19–23)

If we keep this in mind, we find that the irony of some episodes is
intensified. The Priest in *Tratado* II, a man who should relieve the
poor and the suffering, behaves like Dives, begrudging Lazarillo
even the crumbs from his table (until he thinks mice have contami-
nated the loaves). In *Tratado* III, the Squire, who should be a rich
man and who pretends to be one, is worse off than Lazarillo,
since he cannot even beg, and has to depend on a beggar's gifts. In
both these instances, the reversal of expected roles vis-à-vis Lazarillo sheds an ironic light on sectors of sixteenth-century Spanish
society.

The implications of this are also important for the plan of the
work as a whole. Lazarillo begins as Lazarus, as the poor and
suffering beggar, with a good deal of emphasis on the necessity of
making his own way to the top. He ends with what he regards as

---

11 The resemblance between Lazarus and the word-family of *laceria*, *lacerar* etc.
is fortuitous – see Yakov Malkiel, "La familia léxica *lazerar*, *laz(d)rar*, *lazeria*",
Nueva Revista de Filología Hispánica, VI (1952), 209–76.

wealth, "en la cumbre de toda buena fortuna" (7. 80–1), whatever we think of it; but in taking on the money that he lacked, he has also taken on the complacency, the moral insensitivity, of the rich man. This remains true even if, as Truman says, he indulges in "humorous ironical posturing as he recounts his career" (*40*, p. 605), since that would simply add an element of intellectual smugness. If there is something wrong with Lázaro's position, he, like Dives, refuses to recognize it (7. 64–75). The reversal is complete: Lazarus has become Dives. There is tragic irony here, for the height of good fortune, the success which has been bought at so terrible a price, is both precarious (it depends on the constancy of the Archpriest's lust) and squalid (the post of *pregonero* was the lowest and most despised of *oficios reales*; see *16*, p. 67).

There is another Lazarus in the Gospels: the man raised from the dead. Until recently, most critics were unwilling to see any connection between him and Lazarillo: for instance, "Lazaro's namesake is, of course, not the resurrected Lazarus of John XI".[12] This attitude, however, is now less common, and the relevance of John xi to *Lazarillo de Tormes* is recognized by Guillén (*10*, pp. 27–8 and 136), Gilman (*22*, p. 161), Perry (*33*, p. 141), and Concha (*19*, p. 245). It is, indeed, hard to see how sixteenth-century readers, to whom the resurrected Lazarus was as familiar as Lazarus the poor man, could overlook the double connotation of the protagonist's name:

> Now a certain man was sick, named Lazarus, of Bethany, the town of Mary and her sister Martha. . . . Then when Jesus came, he found that he had lain in the grave four days already. . . . Jesus therefore again groaning in himself cometh to the grave. It was a cave, and a stone lay upon it. Jesus said, take ye away the stone. Martha, the sister of him that was dead, saith unto him, Lord, by this time he stinketh: for he hath been dead four days. Jesus saith unto her, Said I not unto thee, that, if thou wouldest believe, thou shouldest see the glory of God? Then they took away the stone from the place where the dead was laid. And Jesus lifted up his eyes, and said, Father, I thank thee that thou hast heard me. And I knew that thou hearest me always: but

---

[12] Robert Alter, *Rogue's Progress: studies in the picaresque novel* (Harvard Studies in Comparative Literature, XXVI, Cambridge, Mass., 1964), p. 2. Cejador had suggested the double Biblical origin of the name half a century before (*9*, p. 17).

because of the people which stand by I said it, that they may
believe that thou hast sent me. And when he thus had spoken, he
cried with a loud voice, Lazarus, come forth. And he that was
dead came forth, bound hand and foot with graveclothes: and
his face was bound about with a napkin. Jesus saith unto them,
Loose him, and let him go.

(John xi. 1, 17, 38–44)

The link is strengthened by Lázaro's description of his sufferings
after being beaten by the Priest: "De lo que sucedió en aquellos
tres días siguientes ninguna fe daré, porque los tuve en el vientre de
la ballena" (2. 352–3). The reference is to an Old Testament narrative – "Now the Lord had prepared a great fish to swallow up
Jonah. And Jonah was in the belly of the fish three days and three
nights" (Jonah i. 17) – but also to its New Testament implications.
The parallel with the resurrection of Christ would have been obvious even if it had not been pointed out in Christ's own prophecy:
"For as Jonas was three days and three nights in the whale's belly;
so shall the Son of man be three days and three nights in the heart
of the earth" (Matthew xii. 40).[13] It is not necessary to conclude that
Lazarillo is being equated with Christ; what matters is the
emphasis on death and resurrection.

This throws some additional light on a key episode of *Tratado*
III. The Squire's house has been described in terms also appropriate
to a grave:

> entramos en casa; la cual tenía la entrada obscura y lóbrega de tal
> manera que parece que ponía temor a los que en ella entraban . . .
> consideraba aquel tener cerrada la puerta con llave ni sentir
> arriba ni abajo pasos de viva persona por la casa. Todo lo que yo
> había visto eran paredes. . . . (3. 45–7 and 62–4)

This prepares us for the story of the corpse (3. 405–20), in which
Lazarillo meets a funeral procession, and, misunderstanding the
widow's lamentations, thinks that the corpse is being taken to the
Squire's house; he flees in abject terror. Riquer (*14*, p. 96) finds
this episode out of character, and decides that it was included
because it was a traditional joke (this has been confirmed by its

---

[13] See *33*, pp. 145–6, though I do not agree with all the conclusions that Perry
draws.

discovery in an Arabic story; see *15*, pp. 58–65), and because the author wanted to stress the poverty of the house. This is true, but the recollection of Lazarus-risen-from-the-dead gives an added poignancy to the scene. Popular belief in the late Middle Ages held the grave to be so dreadful that the resurrected Lazarus "lived in continual misery and horror",[14] so, given the persistence of many medieval attitudes in sixteenth-century Spain, the episode may not, from one point of view, be out of character after all.

More important than this, however, are the clear statements that Lazarillo is given new life by the Blind Man:

> Y fue ansí, que después de Dios éste me dio la vida, y siendo ciego me alumbró y adestró en la carrera de vivir.   (1. 106–7)
> Mas como yo este oficio le hobiese mamado en la leche, quiero decir que con el gran maestro el ciego lo aprendí ...   (3. 243–4)

God gave him life in the first instance, but the Blind Man, replacing his parents, gave him worldly life, worldly knowledge, without which he could not have survived long in the world as he found it.

From the Blind Man he learned not only tricks but total self-centredness that took some time to dominate his character, but that eventually and implacably brought him to what he describes as the height of his ambitions. Yet this new life is really a lowering, not a raising: it is moral death in worldly life, and we witness a disturbing parody of resurrection. The episode of the Salamanca bull, with its comic ambiguity (see p. 48, below), is significant here, since, apart from its other functions in the story, it shows the Blind Man as an ambiguous prophet, a factor of some importance when we consider the care that the author takes to link his prophecies with the end of the book (this is further emphasized in the interpolations of the Alcalá edition). The Blind Man's teaching gives Lazarillo worldly life, and he prophesies his ultimate success, but the teaching and the prophecies are true only on one level; and by following the path mapped out for him, Lazarillo reaches the moral squalor in which we leave him at the end of the book.

If, then, the validity of the Biblical reminiscences is accepted,

---

[14] J. Huizinga, *The Waning of the Middle Ages*, trans. F. Hopman (1924, repr. Harmondsworth: Penguin, 1955), p. 148.

we see a character who turns from Lazarus into Dives, and who is apparently raised from worldly death to worldly life, but is in reality plunged from moral life into moral death. The two aspects of Lazarus point in the same direction.

4 Structure

The formal structure of *Lazarillo de Tormes* is simple and obvious: a Prologue and seven *tratados*. Since *Tratados* II, III, IV and V each deal with Lazarillo's life with one master, and since these occupy about two-thirds of the book, it is easy to form the impression that the division made by the author is natural and inevitable, with one *tratado* for each master.[1] This is, however, an over-simplification, since *Tratado* I also includes Lazarillo's life with his parents, VI deals briefly with two masters, and VII covers the eighth master, Lázaro's first independent post, and the Archpriest. There is, then, something slightly arbitrary about the author's choice of a sevenfold division, and it may have been unconsciously governed by the powerful attraction of the number seven in folklore (e.g. the seventh son of a seventh son) and in Christian tradition (e.g. the seven deadly sins, the seven days of Creation). A numerical structure of this kind (three and five are also powerful folkloric and religious numbers) is frequent in medieval and Renaissance literature; sometimes it has symbolic value, but that does not seem to be the case in *Lazarillo*.[2]

The picaresque novel is characteristically episodic in structure: a series of episodes is arranged in a more or less arbitrary fashion, and the chief unifying factor is the appearance in all of them of the same protagonist. For this reason, the workings of Fortune (seen as mere chance, not as Providence) determine many of the incidents, and unmotivated, usually squalid, accidents occupy a large part of most picaresque novels (see 3, pp. 28–39; significantly, this section does not mention *Lazarillo*). Most of the episodes in most of the novels could be omitted or transposed without effecting any fundamental change. It is true that usually there is also some

---

[1] It has sometimes been suggested that the division into *tratados*, and therefore the choice of headings, is due not to the author but to the first printer. Most of the book's recent critics, however, rightly believe this division to be part of the original work.

[2] There are critics who take a different view, e.g. Fred Abrams, "A Note on the Mercedarian Friar in the *LT*", *Romance Notes*, XI (1969–70), 444–6.

development of plot (leading, for example, to the protagonist's
reintegration with society), and that in the best picaresque novels
a tighter structure can be discerned, but the general impression
given by almost all of these novels is nevertheless that of a largely
random accumulation of incidents. It is less easy to form such an
impression of the *Buscón* and of *Guzmán de Alfarache* : as recent
criticism has shown, their episodic and random nature is merely
superficial.[3] The difference between the structure of *Lazarillo de
Tormes* and that of most picaresque novels is even clearer : many
episodes could be transposed only at the cost of destroying the
novel's pattern (*Tratados* IV and V, and V and VI, are inter-
changeable, but IV and VI could not easily be transposed, and I,
II and III have to occur in their present order). Moreover, the book
rapidly becomes less episodic : *Tratado* I can be subdivided without difficulty, but the other long *tratados* (II, III and the rather
shorter V) all have their own coherent plots, and cannot be split
into autonomous incidents. Perhaps most important of all, the
episodes bring about a change in Lazarillo's character as well as in
his economic circumstances; this approaches the interaction of plot
and character found in what Edwin Muir calls the dramatic novel,[4]
and it may well owe something to the influence of *La Celestina*.

The less episodic nature of *Lazarillo* is, of course, partly to be
explained by its chronological position : the author of what we
now see as the first picaresque novel had no way of knowing what
the norms for the genre would be. The models to which he could
turn were, with one exception, either much less coherent structurally, or much more so. Folktales, to which, as we shall see,
Lazarillo is indebted for much of its content, have their own structure, but in the mid-sixteenth century the only way in which
writers were accustomed to combine them was the loose organiza-
tion of the jest-book and its medieval ancestor the *exemplum* col-

---

[3] See, for instance, Francisco Rico, "Estructuras y reflejos de estructuras en el
Guzmán de Alfarache", *MLN*, LXXXII (1967), 171–84; C. B. Morris, *The Unity
and Structure of Quevedo's Buscón: desgracias encadenadas* (Occasional Papers in
Modern Languages, I, Hull : Univ., 1965).

[4] Muir's *The Structure of the Novel* (Hogarth Lectures on Literature, VI, London : Hogarth, 1928) is often underestimated by hispanists because its treatment of
the picaresque novel (pp. 28–33) has obvious defects in a Spanish context; but it
remains the best book in its field.

lection.[5] On the other hand, *La Celestina*, biographies and autobiographies, and the chivalresque romances which *Lazarillo* in
part parodies, are in their different ways based on firm structural
principles. Only *The Golden Ass*, which exists in a Greek version
attributed to Lucian and a Latin version by Apuleius (both written
in the second century, both available in Spanish translation in the
mid-sixteenth), possesses an episodic yet clearly organized structure. Like *Lazarillo*, the work of pseudo-Lucian shows the transi-
tion from poverty to prosperity, and holds this up as an example;
it has been established as one of *Lazarillo*'s more important sources
(see 26, pp. 33–40).

The folkloric origin of some incidents in *Lazarillo* will be discussed in Chapter 8, but there is also the question of a structural
influence. Lázaro Carreter (26, pp. 64–122) has applied to this
novel the research of folklorists (Vladimir Propp and Axel Olrik)
into the structures of popular tales, and he has obtained some most
interesting results. For example, he shows that the graduated
arrangement of Lazarillo's first three masters, with the first exercis-
ing greatest influence and the third exciting the greatest sympathy,
follows Olrik's "Law of Three" together with his law of first and
last positions (26, pp. 98–102). The author seems, from Lázaro
Carreter's findings, to be at once dependent on folktale structure
(when the series of three ends, his creative inspiration seems to tire;
26, pp. 154–6), and independent of it: although individual incidents in *Tratado* I are folkloric, their linking into a causal sequence
is not (26, p. 117; this confirms Lida de Malkiel, 27, p. 358).

If, then, the structure of *Lazarillo* cannot be satisfactorily explained by its formal division into seven *tratados*, by any one literary model, or by the influence of folktales (though each of these
offers a partial explanation), is it possible to identify a structure that
the author devised for himself? I believe that it is. The narrative
begins with Lazarillo's parents, and an apparently stable environment. Growing instability in his home sends him out into the
world, and from his first master he learns the basic lessons with
which he will make his way in society; on the narrative level, this
section is divided into brief episodes. Then come two sections of

5 Stanley J. Kahrl, "The Medieval Origins of the Sixteenth-Century English Jest-
Books", *Studies in the Renaissance*, XIII (1966), 166–83.

extended narrative, in each of which there is a reversal of expected
roles: the Priest withholds charity, the Squire has to be fed by his
servant (3. 327–8; cf. 612–14); in these two sections, the lessons
taught by the Blind Man are supplemented but not fundamentally
altered – in that respect, *Tratados* II and III are a period of con-
solidation. With *Tratados* IV, V, VI and the first part of VII, we
see Lázaro, in a series of brief episodes, applying the lessons and
moving up in society (still at a squalid level, admittedly, but nevertheless moving up). Finally, with Lázaro's marriage we see him
again in a home environment of apparent stability, again dependent on a woman and her lover for food and security,[6] and again
more precariously situated than he realizes (or will allow himself to
realize).

The beginning of *Tratado* I thus balances the last part of VII;
the learning of lessons in brief episodes with the Blind Man
balances their application in the brief episodes of *Tratados* IV–VII;
and in the middle, we have the two extended narratives of lessons
reinforced and roles reversed (II and III). To put it even more
briefly, *Lazarillo de Tormes* consists of six sections which divide
into balancing pairs; or of a series of three sections followed by
another three in reverse order. (Somewhat different structures,
both of them based on a balance of sections, are suggested by
Willis, *44*, p. 277, and Guillén, *10*, p. 29.)

It is far from certain that the author planned all of this at the
conscious level, though he must have been aware of some of the
pattern (see the discussion of parallels, below). What matters, however, is that consciously or unconsciously he imposed a firm structure on his diverse material, and that his structure is not only
aesthetically satisfying but, as we shall see, emphasizes the themes
of the novel. The pattern becomes even clearer if we look beyond
the narrative to the narrator's explanation: the concluding paragraphs, with their reference to "el caso" (7. 65–6) and address to
"vuestra merced" (7. 79), balance the prologue, and lead from the
narrative into the situation that produced it (the enquiries made
by the Archpriest's friend).

The framing technique which we have just observed (Lázaro's

---

[6] This point, like most of the common ground of *Lazarillo* criticism, comes from
Tarr's brilliant pioneer article (*39*).

career framed in the disconcertingly similar domestic settings of *Tratados* I and VII, the whole narrative framed in the Archpriest's friend's concern with "el caso") is used on a smaller scale in *Tratado* I. Indeed, the structure described here for the novel as a whole closely resembles that pointed out by Rico (35, p. 26) for the five principal incidents of Lazarillo's life with the Blind Man: the pillar balances, and is a retaliation for, the bull; the wine and the sausage incidents are similar in planning and in outcome; and these two pairs flank the central incident of the grapes, which is unlike any of them. Looking specifically at the frame, we see that the hostility between the Blind Man and Lazarillo begins with the incident of the stone bull, and, after a series of short episodes, ends with the incident of the pillar. Two heads crash against stone, a cruel trick is repaid by another, Lazarillo's awakening ("en aquel instante desperté de la simpleza en que como niño dormido estaba", 1. 97–8) leads to the Blind Man's near-death ("cayó luego para atrás, medio muerto y hendida la cabeza", 1. 414–15), and the imagery emphasizes the connection (see p. 67, below).

The parallel between Lázaro's initial and final situations may be seen in another way. In one sense, his position has changed for the better: food is more plentiful, security greater, status higher. This is the aspect which he stresses, and early critics were too inclined to accept his valuation. As we have seen, the adult Lázaro's home is very similar to that of the child's in its precarious dependence on a woman and her lover; indeed, the similarities are greater than the differences, though the differences are real enough. The author's technique – the depiction of parallel situations, like yet unlike – owes something to figura, or typology, the method with which the medieval Church established parallels between the Old and New Testaments. A person, place or event in the Old Testament was seen as prefiguring or foreshadowing one in the New Testament, which it resembled in one or more important respects (despite differences in others).[7] Thus, the city of Jerusalem prefigured the Christian Church, and Abraham's willingness to sacrifice Isaac at God's command prefigured the sacrifice of Christ on the Cross. In time, this technique was applied to secular literature. Thus

[7] See Erich Auerbach, "Figura", in *Scenes from the Drama of European Literature* (New York: Meridian, 1959), pp. 11–76.

Lázaro's beginning prefigures his end; his mother prefigures his wife; and, in a different way, Lazarillo's father, who "padeció persecución por justicia" (1. 13), prefigures the adult Lázaro's duty as *pregonero*: "acompañar los que padecen persecuciones por justicia y declarar a voces sus delitos" (7. 16–18) – the implication is that the criminal and the man who denounces him are not so far apart. And there is more to come: an adverse turn of Fortune ("Quiso nuestra fortuna", 1. 44) destroys the security of Lazarillo's childhood home. Are we to take this as prefiguring what will befall him in Toledo? The last sentence of the novel, with the imperfect tense of "estaba en mi prosperidad" and the reference to Fortune (7. 80–1) suggests that we are.[8]

Figura is distinct from the other method of linking the Old and New Testaments, that of prophecy and its fulfilment, but they are sometimes used in conjunction. Here also, *Lazarillo de Tormes* seems to follow precedent. The Blind Man prophesies that "si un hombre en el mundo ha de ser bienaventurado con vino, que serás tú" (1. 366–7), and Lázaro comments that "el pronóstico del ciego no salió mentiroso" (1. 369). He does not explain further, and when he obtains the "cargo de pregonar los vinos que en esta ciudad se venden" (7. 15–16) he does not refer back to the prophecy, but for readers accustomed to this aspect of Biblical commentary (that is, for all sixteenth-century readers), no explicit reminder would be necessary.[9] Prophecy is, of course, not confined to the Bible, and as Lázaro Carreter points out (26, pp. 89–90) it is a frequent element in folklore, but in this case its use in conjunction with figura to link *Tratados* I and VII, and the frequent religious references in the text, both point to a probably Biblical origin.

Figura and prophecy are not the only techniques with which the author establishes parallels between different parts of his novel. Imagery has an important function here (see Chapter 6), as do

---

[8] The prefiguration of Lázaro's end by his beginning is the clearest case of figural technique, but it may not be the only one. It is possible that some other parallels between incidents and between characters are affected by it, but it is often hard to distinguish between a marginal case of secularized figura and the impulse to symmetrical construction found in the literature and art of all periods. In this particular case, it should be noted that Rico has a different explanation for "estaba" (35, pp. 22–3).

[9] The Alcalá interpolator, however, did make the prophecy element more explicit.

repetitions of situations and of phrases, most of which have been noted by previous critics. Each reader can without difficulty make up his own list; what follows is indicative, not exhaustive. Lazarillo's widowed mother "determinó arrimarse a los buenos por ser uno dellos" (1. 20), which means not virtue but advantage. When, therefore, her farewell to her son includes "Procura de ser bueno, y Dios te guíe" (1. 82–3), not even the religious emphasis quite banishes the suspicion that she is urging Lazarillo to seek worldly success. Similar connotations are more clearly seen when Lazarillo tells the Squire that "fuime por esa ciudad a encomendarme a las buenas gentes" (3. 258–9): "buenas gentes" are those who will charitably give him food, but also those who are prosperous enough to have food to give. There is, of course, still room for doubt, but all doubt vanishes when the Archpriest tells Lázaro to put self-interest before the opinion of others (profit before honour), and Lázaro acquiesces. "Señor – le dije – yo determiné de arrimarme a los buenos" (7. 50).[10] *Tratados* I and II are linked by the belief of the Blind Man and the Priest that bad luck has coincided with Lazarillo's arrival: "¿Qué diablo es esto, que después que comigo estás no me dan sino medias blancas, y de antes una blanca y un maravedí hartas veces me pagaban?" (1. 161–3); "¿Qué diremos a esto? ¡Nunca haber sentido ratones en esta casa sino agora!" (2. 243–4). There is a difference in their reactions: the Priest sees, at this stage, merely a coincidence, while the Blind Man, with paradoxically sharper insight, half-suspects Lazarillo.[11]

Tratado III is firmly associated with the beginning of the adult Lázaro's fulfilment of his ambitions, and also with the hollowness of his success. The Squire attaches supreme importance to "los hombres de bien", and to his own membership of that group (3. 89, 263, 468, 474–5), but Lazarillo soon comes to realize that this

[10] The misuse of *bueno* is, as Wardropper shows (*43*), part of a general inversion of moral values in this novel. It is possible that, as Truman suggests (*40*, pp. 602–3), the comic effect of this ambiguous use of *bueno* is intended by Lázaro as well as by the author.

[11] There are other links between *Tratados* II and III, e.g. the gnawing of bones (2. 40–1, 3. 310–11), where stylistic detail confirms and sharpens the general picture of hunger; the choice of *arca*, which dominates Lazarillo's thinking in II, as an image in III ("aquel mendrugo de pan que su criado Lázaro trujo un día y una noche en el arca de su seno", 3. 202–4), as if Lazarillo had turned into the desired object; and see Tarr (*39*, p. 409).

is a sham, and that the Squire's "razonable vestido" (3. 13–14) covers abject poverty and ultimate disgrace. When, however, he manages to save a little money during his four years with the Chaplain he uses it "para me vestir muy honradamente de la ropa vieja"; and "Desque me vi en hábito de hombre de bien", he decides that water-selling is beneath his dignity (6. 12–18). He takes on the Squire's attitude, which in *Tratado* III he ridiculed, when he puts on Squire-like clothes.[12] And he seems to have learned one more lesson: in a crisis, the Squire runs away from his creditors, leaving Lazarillo to suffer the consequences (3. 542–4), and in the first job he takes after becoming an "hombre de bien", Lázaro runs away from danger, leaving the Constable to suffer (7. 3–5). Finally, *Tratado* III is to some extent a rehearsal for the writing of the book. The Squire is the first of Lazarillo's masters to take a human interest in him:

> preguntándome muy por extenso de dónde era y cómo había venido a aquella ciudad; y yo le di más larga cuenta que quisiera . . . Con todo eso, yo le satisfice de mi persona lo mejor que mentir supe, diciendo mis bienes y callando lo demás.
> (3. 52–8)

The adult Lázaro responds similarly when the Archpriest's friend makes a similar request:

> Y pues V. M. escribe se le escriba y relate el caso muy por extenso, parecióme no tomalle por el medio, sino del principio, porque se tenga entera noticia de mi persona.   (*Pr.* 34–6)

We have been warned: the narratives which are alike in their cause and in their length may be alike also in their unreliability.[13]

The use of prophecy as a structural device has already been discussed. Its counterpart is a series of recollections and references back, by the young protagonist and the adult narrator, throughout

---

[12] These similarities are well discussed by Jones (*12*, pp. xxxi–xxxv). C. B. Morris, "Lázaro and the Squire: *hombres de bien*", *BHS*, XLI (1964), 238–41, adds the suggestion that the Squire may be mad. If Morris were right, this would raise a problem, since the generally accepted charge of hypocrisy would collapse.

[13] I do not mean that we should distrust the overt facts of Lázaro's narrative to Vuestra Merced (this question is discussed in Ch. 7). In both cases, omissions and dubious interpretations are likely to be the means of deceit. There is a second auto-biographical narrative in this *tratado*: that of the Squire (3. 466–537), which is also intended to mislead.

the first three *tratados*.[14] When the Blind Man crashes into the
pillar, Lazarillo reminds him of the sausage episode (1. 416), and
the narrator recalls the pillar trick early in *Tratado* II (50–2). The
Blind Man and the Priest are both recalled in 3. 339–41, and
Lazarillo remembers bitterly, when he discovers the extent of the
Squire's poverty, that he had wondered whether he would find a
more miserable existence than that with the Priest (3. 78–80). There
are other instances (2. 5–6, 140, 315; 3. 204; 4. 2), but a particularly
interesting one is "como yo este oficio le hobiese mamado en la
leche, quiero decir que con el gran maestro el ciego lo aprendí"
(3. 243–4), which seems to recall Lazarillo's infancy, but turns out
to be a reference to his days with his first master.

The structure of *Lazarillo de Tormes*, like that of any other
novel, has a number of turning-points. The most important are –
since this is the story of how a child became a corrupt, selfish and
hypocritical adult – two shocks which Lazarillo receives at the
hands of his masters (cf. *3*, p. 61). The first is the more famous: the
episode of the bull, which ends his childhood innocence and teaches
him that the world is full of enemies (1. 91–8). The second and
perhaps worse shock comes not from physical ill-treatment but
from the Squire's desertion. Lazarillo had learned to be vengeful
and secretive, but only in reaction against a hostile environment.
When he meets the Squire, who is well-disposed though unreli-
able, he develops a protective attitude, and betrayal by the master
whom he had come to regard as a friend is shattering. Lazarillo
reaches the depths of despair: "acabé de conocer mi ruin dicha"
(3. 611). After this, self-interest is his only guide. It is perhaps more
than a coincidence that this is immediately followed by a stylistic
shock for the reader: Willis points out that by the end of *Tratado*
III, the reader is closely involved with Lazarillo, and shares his
time-scale, but that the abrupt change of tempo in *Tratado* IV,
with Lazarillo moving swiftly through the context of experience,
establishes a distance between reader and protagonist (*44*,
pp. 274–5; cf. *23*, pp. 275–6).[15]

[14] For the more general question of memory's role in the creation of *Lazarillo*, see
Guillén (*23*), and Dorothy S. Severin, *Memory in La Celestina* (London: Tamesis,
1970), pp. 67–70.
[15] Willis's illuminating argument is restated in different terms by Andrée Collard,
"The Unity of *LT*", *MLN*, LXXXIII (1968), 262–7.

Gradation and climax have long been recognised as a major part of *Lazarillo*'s structural resources. Tarr (39) pointed out that in *Tratado* I, after the episode of the bull, the incidents in the struggle between the Blind Man and Lazarillo show increasing attention to detail and dramatic effect; that hunger dominates the first three *tratados*, reaching a climax in III; that, ironically, hunger worsens as Lazarillo goes up the social scale of masters; that he runs away from the first master, is dismissed by the second and abandoned by the third; and that the subordination of Lazarillo to other characters as the centre of narrative interest, which begins in *Tratado* III (because there is no conflict, we are forced to take an interest in the Squire as a person), reaches a climax in *Tratado* V, where Lazarillo is a mere onlooker. Later critics have been able to expand this list somewhat; for instance, Gilman argues that "the patterned sequence of masters and degrees of starvation is overlaid by another ironical sequence, that of prayer" (22, p. 159).

What is true of the book as a whole, or of long sections within it, can also be true of short sections. The early part of *Tratado* III depends on the building up of a double tension, first of expectation and then of anxiety. Lazarillo's pleasurable expectation of ample food when he first meets the Squire is vividly described (3. 24–41); even the Squire's failure to buy food as they pass through the market helps to convince the boy that there must already be abundant food in the house. The first misgiving, however, is soon to come: the Squire's house "tenía la entrada obscura y lóbrega de tal manera que parece que ponía temor a los que en ella entraban" (3. 46–7; are we intended to recall the gateway to Dante's Hell, with its inscription, "Abandon hope, all ye that enter here"?). This note of fear, which prepares the way for the story of the funeral procession later in the *tratado*, is temporarily offset by the reassuring observation that "dentro della estaba un patio pequeño y razonables cámaras" (3. 48). Then ominous signs reappear, "por ser ya casi las dos y no le ver más aliento de comer que a un muerto" (3. 61–2) – again, there is not only rational misgiving about food, but also a premonition of death which prepares us for the later episode (and, of course, the later episode happens largely because Lazarillo has accustomed himself to thinking of death in connection with his master's house). And all of this is reinforced by "parecía casa encantada" (3. 66; "encantada" here means "under an evil spell").[16]

We have already noticed one type of story-within-the-story, when Lazarillo tells the Squire about his life, and later listens to the Squire's account. Another type is more frequent: the telling of comic stories to neighbours or passers-by. These are usually about Lazarillo's tricks and consequent sufferings, but the word "comic" is appropriate because the stories produce laughter, sometimes even from the victim. Thus:

> si alguno le decía por qué me trataba tan mal, luego contaba el cuento del jarro . . . Santiguándose los que lo oían, . . . reían mucho el artificio. (1. 225–31)
> Contaba el mal ciego a todos cuantos allí se allegaban mis desastres, y dábales cuenta una y otra vez, así de la del jarro como de la del racimo, y agora de lo presente. Era la risa de todos tan grande que toda la gente que por la calle pasaba entraba a ver la fiesta; mas con tanta gracia y donaire recontaba el ciego mis hazañas que, aunque yo estaba tan maltratado y llorando, me parecía que hacía sinjusticia en no se las reír. (1. 342–8)
> Ahí tornaron de nuevo a contar mis cuitas y a reírlas, y yo, pecador, a llorarlas. (2. 370–1)
> Riéronse mucho el alguacil y el escribano, diciendo: "Bastante relación es ésta para cobrar vuestra deuda." (3. 589–90)

This technique does not attain the complexity which we find in some story-within-story structures both before and after *Lazarillo*, but it serves to give depth to the narrative and to vary the viewpoint (see also *20*, pp. 94–6).

To sum up, *Lazarillo de Tormes* appears at first glance to have the episodic structure typical of most later picaresque novels, but when we look more closely we quickly see that, especially from *Tratado* II onwards, it is less episodic than its successors, and that it has a fundamentally linear plot. In this, it resembles the majority of non-picaresque novels. Its structure is tightened by a fairly strong element of causality, by a symmetrical distribution of complementary units, and by thematic links. As Rico says, unity is

---

[16] Expectation is built up again later in the *tratado*, with the Squire's assurances that they will soon leave that unlucky house. This proves to be true, but in a disastrous way: see p. 51, below.

provided by the convergence of all the past episodes on the present *caso*, which the narrator is trying to explain (*13*, p. l; he later compares this structure to that of some short poems, *35*, pp. 31–3; cf. *3*, p. 17). Moreover, this unified structure has a thematic purpose – still an unusual feature in prose fiction by the 1550s, as Lázaro Carreter notes (*26*, pp. 92–4). The themes are interwoven, and like the plot they converge on the *caso* of *Tratado* VII. Indeed, it is on the level of theme, not of plot, that we see the interlace pattern characteristic of the structure of many medieval romances and of some of their sixteenth-century successors.[17] And once plot and themes converge on Lázaro's ill-gotten and precarious success, the book is forever closed. Sequels are out of place – a fact that the Alcalá interpolator uncharacteristically failed to grasp when he added to the final sentence the words "de lo que de aquí adelante me sucediere avisaré a vuestra merced".[18]

---

[17] See Eugène Vinaver, *The Rise of Romance* (Oxford: Clarendon, 1971). This is also to some extent true of the *Buscón* and of *Guzmán de Alfarache*.

[18] See *26*, p. 86. It follows that the sixteenth-century printers and translators (including David Rowland) who attached to the novel, as *Tratado* VIII, the first chapter of the apocryphal 1555 sequel were in error, despite the ingenious arguments of Carlos Ripoll, "El tratado VIII del *Lazarillo*", in *La Celestina a través del decálogo y otras notas sobre la literatura de la Edad de Oro* (New York: Las Américas, 1969), pp. 125–94. The sequel is, however, better than has been supposed, as Richard E. Zwez shows, *Hacia la revalorización de la Segunda parte del Lazarillo (1555)* (Valencia: Albatros, 1970). José Caso González, "La génesis del *LT*", *Archivum*, XVI (1966 [1968]), 129–55, argues that the 1554 *Lazarillo*, the Alcalá interpolations and the 1555 sequel are all based on a much earlier, and hypothetical, *Libro de Lázaro de Tormes*. There has not yet been much discussion of this startling theory, but it seems unlikely to convince most scholars.

5 Style (excluding imagery)

The narrator apologizes at the outset for his "grosero estilo" (*Pr.* 28). This is a traditional formula of humility and self-deprecation, and to that extent need not be taken seriously. *Lazarillo* is not the artless narrative of an uneducated person who simply wants to set down, as best he can, what has happened to him, but rather an artefact carefully planned and polished until it gives to the casual observer the appearance of untutored spontaneity. A few genuinely unpolished autobiographical statements, usually taken down by lawyers, have survived from the fifteenth and sixteenth centuries,[1] and even the briefest comparison of these with *Lazarillo* shows how right modern critics are to reject the narrator's description of his style. Indeed, the *Prólogo* itself, which is consciously literary, makes the description absurd from the start.

Yet, in another sense, "grosero estilo" deserves to be taken seriously, since it reflects a division of subject-matters and styles which dominated medieval and early Renaissance literary theory. This division, known as Virgil's Wheel, classified styles as high, medium and low (*gravis, mediocris, humilis*), each being appropriate to a different kind of subject-matter. The high style was suitable for narrating the deeds of kings, and the low for telling of the lives of humble people. One of the great achievements of medieval literature was to establish, with the Gospels as precedent, that the poor could be written about seriously, even tragically, and that an unadorned style was no obstacle to such treatment.[2] This, however,

---

[1] For example, the *Memorias* of Leonor López de Córdoba (early fifteenth century), ed. Adolfo de Castro, *La España Moderna*, no. 163 (1902), 120–46; and the sixteenth-century Inquisition documents printed by Stephen Gilman, *The Spain of Fernando de Rojas: the intellectual and social landscape of La Celestina* (Princeton: Univ. Press, 1972).

[2] See Erich Auerbach, *Mimesis: the representation of reality in Western literature*, trans. Willard Trask (Princeton: Univ. Press, 1953). This concept is self-evident to us, but in terms of classical Latin literature it is revolutionary. Plebeian characters are presented comically in *Lazarillo*, but so is everyone else (see 35, p. 36).

did not alter the classification of subject and style (*La Celestina*'s
modification of this inflexible linking of stylistic level with the
social class of the characters was not generally adopted until long
afterwards), and *Lazarillo*'s first readers would have thought it
entirely appropriate that a story of low life, described by its narrator as "esta nonada" (*Pr.* 28), should be in the low, or relatively
unadorned, style.

Such a style need not, however, be "grosero" in the full sense,
and in *Lazarillo* it is not. It is colloquial yet worked out with great
care to produce its effects, some of which are extremely subtle. It
is only after several readings that one is likely to appreciate all of
the effects to the full, but this does not mean that a first reading
will be ineffectual. The *Prólogo* says that there is something here
for every type of reader; and at this point we can be fairly sure that
the author, as well as the narrator, is speaking.

One of the stylistic resources exploited in *Lazarillo* is paradox,
sometimes allied to ambiguity, as in "mi nuevo y viejo amo" (1.
77), where the apparent paradox makes sense only because of the
ambiguity of "nuevo" (new to Lazarillo although so old and bat-
tered that he is not new in any other way). Other examples of paradox are "aquel dulce y amargo jarro" (1. 203), "holgábame a mí
de quebrar un ojo por quebrar dos al que ninguno tenía" (1. 236–7)
"el tiempo que con él veví o, por mejor decir, morí" (2. 59–60),
"acabamos de comer, aunque yo nunca empezaba" (2. 191–2), "me
toparon mis pecados con un clérigo" (2. 2–3; paradox is used here
as a vehicle for anti-clerical satire), "me fue forzado sacar fuerzas
de flaqueza" (3. 1), and Lazarillo's prayers that people in his
master's parish might die, so that he might live (2. 68–71 and 83–4).

Ambiguity is a more frequent and more important feature of
this novel's style than paradox, though, as we have seen, they may
operate simultaneously. This is an area in which there is an unusually high risk of error in critical interpretation, since in many
cases one cannot be certain that the meanings which occur to the
critic were intended by the author (at either the conscious or the
subconscious level) or were perceived by his contemporaries. An
example is the use of "caso" in the *Prólogo*: "Y pues V. M. escribe
se le escriba y relate el caso muy por extenso . . ." The primary
meaning is clear: "caso" is the occurrence, the matter. This, how-

ever, may not be the sole meaning.[3] "Caso" is etymologically
related to "caer"; one of the most widely read books of the late
Middle Ages and the Renaissance was Boccaccio's *De casibus
virorum illustrium* (*The Falls of Eminent Men*); and the preoccupation of this period with sudden reversals of fortune, with
falls from Fortune's Wheel, is reflected in the closing words of
Lazarillo, "en este tiempo estaba en mi prosperidad y en la cumbre
de toda buena fortuna" (7. 80–1). The use of "caso" in the *Prólogo*,
only a few lines before a reference to Fortune, may, by the exploitation of ambiguity, contribute to the links between the beginning
and end of the novel (see Ch. 4), and to a more generalized
ambiguity in the ending, which leaves us uncertain of Lázaro's
final position.[4] A less debatable ambiguity occurs with the use of
"fortuna" (*Pr.* 38), a word which recurs several times during the
course of the novel, though never ambiguously. On this first occasion, however, the context seems to affect the meaning. "Fortuna"
could also, when *Lazarillo* was written, mean a storm at sea, and
the reference in the same sentence to "los que, siéndoles contraria,
con fuerza y maña remando, salieron a buen puerto" (*Pr.* 39–40)
would inevitably bring the secondary meaning to mind. "Caso"
and "fortuna" seem, therefore, to form a pattern of interlocking
meanings, dependent on ambiguity, and to give the reader notice
of some of the complexities which await him in the book.

Ambiguity is used humorously at the beginning of the first
tratado: Lazarillo's father has been arrested for stealing corn, "y
confesó y no negó y padeció persecución por justicia. Espero en
Dios que está en la Gloria, pues el Evangelio los llama bienaven-
turados" (1. 12–14; see 22, p. 154). The joke, which seems to have
been borrowed from *La Celestina*, depends on the ambiguity of
"por": in the Beatitudes, it means "for the sake of", but in the

---

[3] It may elsewhere have a slightly different meaning: in 1. 245 it means a
single incident which is chosen as typical. There have occasionally been suggestions
that in the prologue it means a legal case, that Lázaro is awaiting trial, but this
seems unlikely.

[4] The occurrence/fall ambiguity is certainly present in one of the most famous of
late medieval Spanish poems, Juan de Mena's *Laberinto de Fortuna* (1444), still
widely read when *Lazarillo* was published: "Tus casos falaçes, Fortuna, canta-
mos,/estados de gentes que giras e trocas" (stanza 2). The implications of "el caso"
are discussed in *10*, p. 136; *34*, pp. 277–87; and *22*, p. 153.

case of Lazarillo's father it means "at the hands of"; the narrator's
sliding from one meaning to the other is not intended to deceive,
but merely to exploit the comic potential of the word and the situation. A different kind of ambiguity is found in the episode of the
stone bull of Salamanca. The Blind Man says: "Lázaro, llega el
oído a este toro, y oirás gran ruido dentro dél" (1. 89–90). The boy
assumes that "dentro dél" means "inside the bull", but the sentence could equally well mean "inside your ear" (because of a
violent blow), and this is what it turns out to mean. This is the
type of ambiguity traditionally associated with the Delphic Oracle,
which gave to some enquirers apparently reassuring answers but
was later able to point out, quite truthfully, that the answers if read
in a different way foretold disaster. Lazarillo is deceived by this
ambiguity, and suffers a painful awakening: "Parecióme que en
aquel instante desperté de la simpleza en que como niño dormido
estaba" (1. 97–8). This is the first of two major shocks which help
to make the boy into the adult Lázaro; ambiguity is exploited by
the Blind Man for cruel amusement, and by the author for structural development. One more example must suffice: at the end of
the book, Lázaro says that his wife "es tan buena mujer como vive
dentro de las puertas de Toledo" (7. 73–4). At first sight, this is
merely the foolish boast of a man in an untenable position, goaded
by his neighbours until he has to say something. On closer examination, although this first impression remains valid, we see something more. A number of popular tales have as basis the deceptive
oath, as when a queen, rightly suspected of adultery, causes her
lover to disguise himself as a madman and molest her in the street,
whereupon she is able to swear that no man has held her in his
arms save her husband "and that madman whom you saw embrac-
ing me just now". The oath is true in form but false in substance.
Lázaro's assertion may be of this type. He seems to be saying
("sobre la hostia consagrada", 7. 73) that the women of Toledo are
chaste, and that his wife is as chaste as any other, but is he really
saying that he knows his wife is unchaste, and that he strongly
suspects that the other women of Toledo are just as unchaste? We
shall never know for certain. Neither will his neighbours; and
faced with the implications of that ambiguity, it is not surprising
that "Desta manera no me dicen nada" (7. 76).[5]

I have discussed only a few of *Lazarillo*'s ambiguities, which have a variety of functions within the book; others are noted by Truman (*40*). A comprehensive listing and discussion, with a formal classification taking account of William Empson's work,[6] would be instructive but would make the present study too long.

An ironic tone is noticeable throughout this novel, and there are also some specific and localized cases of irony which reinforce the general tone and which convey a message or illuminate an episode. After telling us of the thefts committed by Zaide, his mother's lover, in order to support the family, Lázaro adds:

No nos maravillemos de un clérigo ni fraile, porque el uno hurta de los pobres y el otro de casa para sus devotas y para ayuda de otro tanto, cuando a un pobre esclavo el amor le animaba a esto. (1. 50–4)

This is an allusion to the belief (shared by the courtly and Neoplatonic theories of love in the Middle Ages and Renaissance) that nobility, of character even if not of birth, is essential for true love; but it is also an ironic reversal of the expected position, since it implies that priests are more likely than black slaves to steal in order to maintain their mistresses. Irony is here a weapon of anticlerical satire.

On other occasions, irony has other functions. It may be merely humorous, as with the use of a diminutive or a euphemism for comic understatement: savage blows are "el golpecillo" (1. 208) or "la fiesta" (1. 346). It may, on the other hand, be used primarily to illustrate character, as in the unconscious irony of the Priest's reference to "nuestro pan" (2. 181): as long as the bread was safely in the chest, it was his alone, but once it had gone, the loss was shared. In the third *tratado*, the main function of irony is to emphasize the theme of hunger. When the Squire has eaten the cow-heel supplied by Lazarillo, he says that "me ha sabido como si hoy no hobiera comido bocado" (3. 314–15). He knows that he has in fact

---

[5] Compare the apparently humble understatement of "confesando yo no ser más santo que mis vecinos" (*Pr.* 27-8).

[6] *Seven Types of Ambiguity* (London: Chatto and Windus, 1930; revised ed., 1947). Empson's definition of ambiguity is wide, and includes some stylistic features discussed under other headings in this chapter.

eaten nothing that day, and Lazarillo knows it too, but the social
conventions require that neither should admit this, and irony
allows the fact to be simultaneously concealed and pointed out.
Similarly, when the Squire has laughed at Lazarillo's panic over
the funeral procession, he explains the situation, "desque fue ya
más harto de reír que de comer" (3. 436–7). Since the Squire had
not eaten for some time, it was not difficult for him to be fuller of
laughter than of food, and the ironic description reminds us of his
hunger as well of his amusement. Finally, in the fifth *tratado*,
when the Constable has denounced the Pardoner, the latter prays
to God for justice against "las falsas palabras de aquel hombre"
(5. 93–4). The words are indeed lies, since the Constable, who was
in collusion with the Pardoner, had claimed to be motivated by
righteous indignation in denouncing him, but in another sense
they are true, for the accusations of fraud made by the Constable
are fully justified. Only the two conspirators appreciate the irony
of the Pardoner's phrase, though Lazarillo realizes it later. This
example is related both to the deceitful-oath kind of ambiguity
discussed above, and to what is generally known as dramatic irony.

Dramatic irony, found most often though not exclusively in
plays, involves the use by a character of words whose full import
he does not grasp; words which, to those more alert than the character, foreshadow later and usually disagreeable events. It may be
extended to the use of words which mean one thing to the speaker
and the audience or reader, another to the character addressed.
When the Blind Man finds that a turnip has mysteriously replaced
his sausage, his indignant "¿Qué es esto, Lazarillo?" is met by the
spurious innocence of "¡Lacerado de mí! . . . ¿Si queréis a mí
echar algo?" (1. 311). "Lacerado" here is used figuratively ("poor
wretch"), and is an obvious pun on the name Lazarillo, but it can
also mean, literally, lacerated, as the boy will very shortly be when
his master finds him out. Similarly, Lazarillo's comically exaggerated description of life with the Blind Man and the Priest, and
his belief that it would be practically impossible to find a master in
whose service he would have less to eat, foreshadow the sufferings
of the third *tratado*:

Yo he tenido dos amos: el primero traíame muerto de hambre
y, dejándole, topé con estotro, que me tiene ya con ella en la

sepultura. Pues si deste desisto y doy en otro más bajo, ¿qué será
sino fenecer?   (2. 96–9)

He will, of course, find worse, and while with the Squire he reflects
ruefully that his worst imaginings, never seriously intended, have
come true (3. 78–80, cf. 3. 326–8). This instance of dramatic irony
is perhaps a little obvious; the mechanism is too clearly displayed.
More impressive is an instance in *Tratado* III, partly because we
cannot be sure how far the speaker realizes what his words mean.
The Squire tells Lazarillo that the house he has rented is an unlucky one; "mas yo te prometo, acabado el mes, no quede en ella
aunque me la den por mía" (3. 276–7), and he twice returns to the
point (3. 381–2 and 391–2). The natural meaning of his words –
and probably the only one he intends – is that at the end of the
month he and Lazarillo will move to a better house, but when the
end of the month comes, the Squire, lacking money for the rent,
vanishes, leaving his serving-boy to face the creditors. What Lazarillo, and probably his master, had seen as a promise of better times
to come turns out to be a pointer to yet worse humiliation and
misery. Probably his master, but not definitely: we are bound to
ask ourselves how often the Squire had fled from his debts, and
how long before the fateful day he had taken his decision to abandon his servant. Was Lazarillo the first of his servants to be in this
position? This is one more in the list of problems with which this
enigmatic novel confronts its readers.

Some of the instances of paradox, ambiguity and irony in *Lazarillo* are primarily comic, but others are not. Parody of religious
and secular texts and traditions, which is concentrated in the
Prólogo and the first two *tratados*, is consistently a humorous device which, in contrast with its use in some other works, here has
very little satirical purpose. The *Prólogo* opens with a commonplace of prefatory writings, especially those of chronicles: the
writer's duty to ensure that great deeds are preserved for posterity:

Yo por bien tengo que cosas tan señaladas, y por ventura nunca
oídas ni vistas, vengan a noticia de muchos y no se entierren en
la sepultura del olvido.   (Pr. 1–3)[7]

---

[7] This aim is inconsistent with the claim (Pr. 32–6) that Lázaro is writing a letter
to one person (see p. 78 below).

This would be appropriate to a chronicle of a king's reign, or to one of the sequels to *Amadís de Gaula*, but it is hilariously inappropriate to the story that the narrator will unfold for us. The novel's early readers would not see the point until they had read a few paragraphs of the first *tratado*, but thereafter they would be alert to the parodic possibilities of the book. The title itself, *La vida de Lazarillo de Tormes y de sus fortunas y adversidades*, is what one might expect in a chivalresque romance, and the parodic relationship to these romances, then at the height of their popularity,[8] has been widely noticed by critics (for a dissenting view, see *16*, p. 58). The name Lazarillo de Tormes, which seems to us typically picaresque because of such later novels as *Guzmán de Alfarache* and *Marcos de Obregón*, would to the book's first readers have been an obvious imitation of such names as Amadís de Gaula, Lisuarte de Grecia, and Florisel de Niquea. The form is the same, but a moment's reflection would show readers that all was not well: Lazarillo has connotations different from those of Amadís or Florisel, and the River Tormes is not Gaul or Greece. The parody goes further: Lazarillo's origins, like those of Amadís, are mysterious; like Amadís, he emerges new-born from the water (1. 8–10); his father, exiled from his homeland, dies in a heroic venture (1. 14–18), but "con cargo de acemilero" (1. 17); the Blind Man's grotesque search for the stolen sausage, whose outcome is described in nauseating detail, is then referred to as "la demanda" (1. 355), which had several shades of meaning but would almost inevitably recall *La demanda del Santo Grial*; and the Priest's bread-chest is compared to "corazas viejas de otro tiempo" (2. 257). Finally, Lázaro's threat to fight to the death against anyone who queries his wife's virtue (7. 74–5) is a parodic echo of a knight's duels on his lady's behalf. This recurrent parody of the chivalresque romances, from the first page to the last, is especially appropriate to a novel whose longest chapter is devoted to the absurd pretensions of the Squire.

The chivalresque romances are probably the most frequent object of parody, but they are not alone. Lazarillo's reverential attitude to the bread – "como vi el pan, comencélo de adorar, no

8 See Maxime Chevalier's pamphlet, *Sur le Public du roman de chevalerie* (Bordeaux: Institut d'Etudes Ibériques et Ibéro-Américaines, 1968).

osando recebillo" (2. 151–2) – has overtones of the Mass, but also of the language of the courtly love poetry in the fifteenth and early sixteenth-century *cancioneros*.[9] Biblical texts are also parodied: the brief account of the arrest and punishment of Lazarillo's father, discussed above in the section on ambiguity, is couched in terms mainly borrowed from the New Testament. What is said in St John's Gospel about John the Baptist is here applied to the father's confession (1. 12), and, as we have already seen, a passage from the Beatitudes is used in pseudo-justification of him (1. 13–14).

Another humorous technique – this time one that is shared with the visual arts – is comic exaggeration of a physical detail. The Blind Man's nose, in search of the sausage, "a aquella sazón con el enojo se había aumentado un palmo" (1. 323–4), a detail which might have come from one of the fantasy paintings of Hieronymus Bosch (c. 1459–1516). Similarly, though less strikingly, Lazarillo's mouth is said to have enlarged its capacity remarkably: "la tenía tan hecha bolsa, que me acaeció tener en ella doce o quince maravedís, todo en medias blancas, sin que me estorbasen el comer" (2. 312–14). Not all exaggeration in the novel is primarily humorous. Some, though implausible, is intended to add emphasis. For instance: "A cabo de tres semanas que estuve con él, vine a tanta flaqueza que no me podía tener en las piernas de pura hambre" (2. 45–6), although the narrative of the succeeding paragraphs shows that Lazarillo moved about without difficulty in the service of his master. The Priest's miserliness is stressed by the statement that he borrowed from his neighbours not only a mousetrap but also the cheese-rinds for bait (2. 267–8).

Three other comic techniques deserve mention. First, the qualifying of a statement, ostensibly in the interests of greater precision, but in fact to draw attention to the comic inadequacy of a set phrase or to the humour of a situation. Thus, "aquel día, añadiendo la ración del trabajo de mis manos, o de mis uñas, por mejor decir" (2. 190–1);[10] and Lazarillo's depredations in the bread-chest are referred to as the work of "la culebra (o culebro,

[9] It is now clear that this love was by no means as chaste as the language of its poets might at first suggest, but that does not affect the question of parody.

[10] The implications here are very different from the dehumanizing references to the Squire's "uñas", discussed in the next chapter.

por mejor decir)" (2. 304). Secondly, the puns on "Lazarillo . . .
lacerado" (1. 310–11), "probar" (2. 349), "tarde" (3. 543–5), and
"reverendos . . . reverendas" (5. 16–17). Thirdly, the use of anti-
climax or bathos. The most elaborate example is the Squire's
description of what his estate would be worth if only . . . :

> Mayormente – dijo – que no soy tan pobre que no tengo en mi
> tierra un solar de casas, que a estar ellas en pie y bien labradas,
> diez y seis leguas de donde nací, en aquella costanilla de Valla-
> dolid, valdrían más de docientas veces mil maravedís, según se
> podrían hacer grandes y buenas; y tengo un palomar que, a no
> estar derribado como está, daría cada año mas de docientos palo-
> minos.   (3. 495–501)

In other words, the property is worthless and almost non-existent,
but this truth dawns on the reader only gradually, until what is a
factual anti-climax becomes a humorous climax. There is a com-
parably bathetic filling-in of detail when Lazarillo has attained "el
primer escalón que yo subí para venir a alcanzar buena vida":
after four years, he is dressed "muy honradamente", but the catch
follows immediately, since he dresses

> de la ropa vieja, de la cual compré un jabón de fustán viejo y un
> sayo raído de manga tranzada y puerta, y una capa que había
> sido frisada . . .   (6. 13–15)

His new-found honourable prosperity is shown to have little more
substance than the Squire's estate. Even when he has advanced
further, the enthusiastic account of his "oficio real" (7. 8–13) is
followed by a paragraph which actually describes the post and
shows it to be at a very low level (7. 15–18; on these two passages,
see *40*, pp. 604–5). The fact that the narrator punctures his own
pretensions with the same technique as he uses against the Squire
suggests that, corrupt though the adult Lázaro undoubtedly is,
there may be a little more to be said in his favour than some recent
critics would allow.

Syntactical and conceptual balance, either straightforward or
antithetical, helps to make *Lazarillo*'s style both attractive and
effective. It may be concentrated in a few words ("quise mal al mal
ciego", 1. 212, in which the balance is used as justification for
Lazarillo's vengeful attitude), or it may affect two or more clauses:

"considerando que a pocos golpes tales el cruel ciego ahorraría de mí, quise yo ahorrar dél" (1. 219–20); "Allí se me representaron de nuevo mis fatigas, y torné a llorar mis trabajos" (3. 76–7). Antithetical balance gives an economical and concentrated picture of the battle of wits between the Priest and Lazarillo ("cuantos él tapaba de día, destapaba yo de noche", 2. 250–1) and of its outcome ("Ahí tornaron de nuevo a contar mis cuitas y a reírlas, y yo, pecador, a llorarlas", 2. 370–1). In one case it is combined with physical phrases,[11] as in "al uno de mano besada y al otro de lengua suelta" (3. 340–1), to characterize Lazarillo's first two masters. The antithetical technique may on occasion be much more complex: "Cuando por bien no le tomaban las bulas, buscaba cómo por mal se las tomasen, y para aquello hacía molestias al pueblo e otras veces con mañosos artificios" (5. 20–2). The first half of the sentence (general statement) is balanced by the second half (greater detail), and each half is an antithesis. The associated technique of chiasmus is also used, though less frequently: "puesto Dios ante mis ojos y la lengua en su nombre" (3. 241).

A conceptual feature of *Lazarillo*'s style which has some affinity with antithetical balance is the transfer of qualities. The Blind Man's bread-bag takes on its owner's avarice ("el avariento fardel", 1. 149–50), and when the Blind Man frustrates Lazarillo's attempts to steal the wine, he, not Lazarillo, receives the epithet of "traidor" (1. 177).[12] The reader feels that moral values are beginning to elude his grasp; the local stylistic detail reflects and reinforces a general effect of the book, which Wardropper has called "el trastorno de la moral" (*43*). Physical objects may behave in a similar way. *Blancas* are halved in value (1. 153–63), a sausage becomes a turnip (1. 299–308), and a mouse becomes a snake (*Tratado* II, culminating in 2. 350–1). These transformations, however, are explicitly shown as the result of Lazarillo's trickery; in each case, the mechanism of the trick is carefully explained. For this reason, even if the Blind Man and the Priest begin to feel that surface reality, which they

---

[11] Phrases which use parts of the body for emphasis or vividness, sometimes adding nothing to the literal meaning, as in "llorar de los ojos". See C. C. Smith and J. Morris, "On 'Physical' Phrases in Old Spanish Epic and other Texts", *Proceedings of the Leeds Philosophical and Literary Society, Literary and Historical Section*, XII (1967), 129–90.

[12] See also *1*, p. 46; *2*, p. 70; *29*, pp. 559–60; and Ch. 4, note 11, above.

have trusted all their lives, is beginning to betray them, we do not share their feeling; the only kind of physical transformation which does not depend on an obvious mechanism is the dehumanizing of characters by the use of animal imagery (discussed in the following chapter), and this is such a well-established technique that it does not affect our general view of reality. The impression we receive from *Lazarillo* is therefore very different from that given by some later works of the Golden Age, such as Quevedo's *Sueños* and Gracián's *Criticón*, where hardly anything is what it seems.[13]

This is perhaps the best place to deal with another stylistic feature which involves unexpected shifts, the use of tenses. On many occasions, actions in the past are described not in the imperfect or the preterite but in the present tense. This use of a historic present is a widely accepted method of lending greater vividness and immediacy to a narrative, and is found in literature of all periods, and in ordinary speech. In *Lazarillo*, however, the historic present alternates with imperfect or preterite within the same passage of narrative :

> Levantéme muy quedito y, habiendo en el día pensado lo que había de hacer y dejado un cuchillo viejo que por allí andaba en parte do le hallase, voyme al triste arcaz, y por do había mirado tener menos defensa le acometí con el cuchillo, que a manera de barreno dél usé.   (2. 226–30; cf. 1. 405–6, 3. 212–15)

The tenses may be differently arranged : historic present, preterite, imperfect (3. 165–9), or present, imperfect, preterite, present (3. 416–17). Much the same kind of alternation is found in the Spanish epics and ballads, where it has been the subject of considerable study,[14] though no agreement has yet been reached by scholars on its origin and purpose. This feature of *Lazarillo*'s style is presumably related to the equivalent feature in epic and ballad, but the nature of the relationship has still to be clarified. That problem,

---

[13] See R. D. F. Pring-Mill, "Spanish Golden Age Prose and the Depiction of Reality", *Anglo-Spanish Society Quarterly Review*, no. 32–3 (April-Sept. 1959), 20–31, and "Some Techniques of Representation in the *Sueños* and the *Criticón*", *BHS*, XLV (1968), 270–84. For *Lazarillo*, see *43*, pp. 446–7; *35*, pp. 35–44. Concha (*19*, pp. 259 and 265) refers solely to a moral "engaño a los ojos".

[14] For example, Thomas Montgomery, "Narrative Tense Preference in the *Cantar de Mio Cid*", *Romance Philology*, XXI (1967–8), 253–74; Joseph Szertics, *Tiempo y verbo en el romancero viejo* (Madrid : Gredos, 1967).

however, does not alter the fact that the use of the historic present adds to the effectiveness of the narrative.[15]

An exhaustive account of *Lazarillo's* style would include an examination of such features as the use of synonyms (3. 433, 5. 182), tautology (2. 66), euphemism (3. 217), alliteration (2. 160, 3. 291), and polysyndeton, the repeated use of conjunctions (3. 165–7), and would study their effectiveness, but this chapter makes no claim to be exhaustive, and it seems better to devote the rest of it to some aspects of an important and rather neglected subject, the use of rhetoric in this novel. Rhetoric has a bad name today; to most people, it connotes artificiality and pomposity, though if it is re-labelled as the art of more effective speaking and writing it is still in favour. The more formal devices of rhetoric, however, do not loom as large in modern literature as in the literature of the Middle Ages or Golden Age, when it was a widely-taught subject in schools and universities, and rhetorical treatises of various kinds had great authority.[16] Even apparently simple works – even works whose authors apologized for their "grosero estilo" – were likely to make extensive use of rhetoric. There is, of course, a difficulty here : rhetoric is for the most part a codification and intensification of ordinary speech habits, and any written work, any speech, will contain some elements that can be classified according to the rhetorical treatises, even if the writer or speaker has never heard of rhetoric. This is a real difficulty, but not a major one, since an author trained in rhetoric will normally show a perceptibly higher level of rhetorical usage, and some of the less common devices can, even if not specially obtrusive in his work, be traced with reasonable certainty to his training. A full investigation of the rhetorical features of *Lazarillo* would be extremely useful; what follows is intended only as a preliminary sketch.

[15] The question of present and imperfect tenses in *Tratado* VII (discussed in Ch. 7, below) is probably unconnected with the use of the historic present.

[16] Scholarship on this subject is extensive : see James J. Murphy, *Medieval Rhetoric: a select bibliography* (Toronto : Univ. Press, 1972). A useful introduction is given by Charles S. Baldwin, *Medieval Rhetoric and Poetic (to 1400), interpreted from representative works* (New York : Macmillan, 1928), and *Renaissance Literary Theory and Practice: classicism in the rhetoric and poetry of Italy, France and England* (New York : Columbia Univ. Press, 1939). Most of the important treatises have been translated into English. The precise channels through which a knowledge of rhetorical devices reached writers of different periods are still a matter of scholarly disagreement.

The rhetorical treatises of the Renaissance coincide in most respects with those of the Middle Ages, but in some ways diverge from them and revert to classical models. The chief differences are the advocacy of brevity as a stylistic ideal, and of moderation in the use of some of the more obtrusive rhetorical figures.[17] Not all writers followed the new precepts, and since medieval and Renaissance theory coincide much more often than they diverge, it is convenient to use the medieval terminology which was still familiar to most Spanish writers in the first half of the sixteenth century (for a differently based treatment of *Lazarillo*'s rhetoric, see 6, pp. 41–4).

A fairly typical classification adopted by the medieval treatises is: techniques of amplification; difficult ornaments of style (chiefly imagery of different types, though the distinction between difficult and easy ornaments is to some extent arbitrary); easy ornaments of style, divided into those of language and those of thought.[18] Among the devices of amplification is *oppositum*, saying a thing twice over by making a statement and then denying its opposite. A complex form of this device is used in *Lazarillo*: "A los vecinos despertaba con el estruendo que hacía, y a mí no me dejaba dormir" (2. 290–1). Here *oppositum* is varied by the use of different objects in the two clauses, but the basic principle of statement ("despertaba") and negation of opposite ("no dejaba dormir") is preserved. Devices of amplification are not as frequent in *Lazarillo* as in some works, since the novel was written in a period when brevity was a stylistic ideal, and its concision, always present, is sometimes very noticeable. Of the prescribed techniques of abbreviation, however, *Lazarillo* seems to make frequent use only of past and present participles in place of subordinate clauses (cf. *13*, p. lxxii).

Ornatus difficilis includes not only metaphor and other types of imagery (discussed in Ch. 6) but also *superlatio* (exaggeration,

---

[17] On the fashion for brevity in the late fifteenth and early sixteenth centuries, see Keith Whinnom, "Diego de San Pedro's Stylistic Reform", *BHS*, XXXVII (1960), 1–15, and *Diego de San Pedro* (New York: Twayne, 1974), pp. 84–6 and 113–16; A. C. Spearing, *Criticism and Medieval Poetry* (2nd ed., London: Arnold, 1972), Ch. VII. Whinnom deals also with the reduced use of some rhetorical figures.

[18] This classification is found in, among others, an influential work now available in a good translation: Geoffrey of Vinsauf, *Poetria nova* (circa 1200), trans. Margaret F. Nims (Toronto: Pontifical Institute of Mediaeval Studies, 1967).

discussed above), and *pronominatio,* in which a famous person represents a quality: "porque era el ciego para con éste un Alejandre Magno, con ser la mesma avaricia" (2. 8–9; cf. 3. 222). Alexander the Great had, in secular literature, a reputation for liberality,[19] and to say that the Blind Man, though avarice personified, nevertheless seems as generous as Alexander when one compares him with the Priest, implies unimaginable depths of meanness in Lazarillo's second master. This sentence is a good example of the way in which the author uses the resources offered him by the rhetorical tradition: he combines *pronominatio* and straightforward personification ("con ser la mesma avaricia") to produce a grotesquely exaggerated effect (*superlatio*). There is seldom anything mechanical about the use of rhetoric in *Lazarillo*; far more often, apparently simple effects are obtained by the skilful use of complex resources.

Among the figures of language usually included by the rhetorical treatises in the category of *ornatus facilis* are *correctio,* the qualifying of a statement for greater precision (discussed above as a comic device); *repetitio,* the repetition of a word at the same point in successive clauses ("Allí se me representaron . . ., allí se me vino . . ., allí lloré", 3. 76–81); and two devices which employ related, or apparently related, words. The first of these, *annominatio,* involves conceptual play on words from the same etymological base, or words which look and sound very similar: "Yo torné a jurar y perjurar" (1. 316), "vime tan maltratado que luego sospeché mi mal" (2. 362–3), "nunca osé desmandarme a demandar" (3. 362). *Annominatio* is at one extreme closely related to the pun, and at the other cannot easily be distinguished from *traductio,* which involves the use of two or more words from the same root (noun and verb, participle and finite verb, infinitive and finite verb, and so on), but which normally lacks the element of conceptual play. *Traductio* is very frequent in *Lazarillo,* as in many other works of this period, but it never reaches the exaggerated level sometimes found in the chivalresque romances of Feliciano de Silva and parodied by Cervantes in the "razón de la sinrazón" passage of

---

[19] George Cary, *The Medieval Alexander* (Cambridge: Univ. Press, 1956), especially Appendix II.

Don Quijote.[20] Typical examples are: "las malas burlas que el
ciego burlaba de mí" (1. 375), "pareciéndome con aquel remedio
remediar" (2. 132–3), "Tanta lástima haya Dios de mí como yo
había dél, porque sentí lo que sentía, y muchas veces había por ello
pasado y pasaba cada día" (3. 282–4), and "el más desenvuelto y
desvergonzado y el mayor echador dellas [las bulas] que jamás yo
vi ni ver espero ni pienso que nadie vio" (5. 1–3); in the last case,
traductio is used for climactic emphasis.

Figures of thought make up the other part of *ornatus facilis*.
Those used in *Lazarillo* include *similitudo* (the easier type of
image, chiefly similes), *contentio* (antithetical balance, discussed
above), and *diminutio* (understatement, discussed above in its
ironic function).

Lazarillo's debt to the rhetorical tradition is not confined to
devices of amplification and stylistic ornament; it also includes a
number of *topoi* (commonplaces) widely used in the Middle Ages
and Renaissance.[21] Discussion of *topoi* in Spanish literature has
become unduly heated in recent years, since some critics feel that
to indicate an author's use of a *topos* is to accuse him of insincerity.
This is not so: *topoi* arose from real feelings and ideas, whose frequency or striking nature led to their formulation in more or less
standard terms. A *topos* may, therefore, express an author's real
position, or it may be mere convention; the question can be
answered only by a study of the individual context, if at all.

Prologues are especially rich in *topoi*, and *Lazarillo*'s is no exception.[22] The first sentence combines two *topoi*: the duty to pre-
serve knowledge of famous deeds, and novelty ("cosas tan seña-

[20] The rhetorical treatises warn against exaggerated use of *traductio*. Those of
the Middle Ages are more tolerant of *annominatio* than those of the Renaissance,
and *Lazarillo*'s relative fondness for *annominatio* and *traductio* shows – as does its
restricted use of the techniques of abbreviation – that its rhetoric is not as thorough
ly humanistic as Diego de San Pedro's in the *Cárcel de Amor*.

[21] The fundamental study is Ernst R. Curtius, *European Literature and the Latin
Middle Ages*, trans. Willard R. Trask (London: Routledge, 1953).

[22] For prologues of this period, see Alberto Porqueras-Mayo, *El prólogo en el
Renacimiento español* (*Revista de Literatura*, anejo XXIV, Madrid, 1965), and
Joseph L. Laurenti, *Los prólogos en las novelas picarescas españolas* (Madrid:
Castalia, 1971). The rhetorical structure of prologues and their use of *topoi* are
thoroughly dealt with by Heinrich Lausberg, *Manual de retórica literaria: funda-
mentos de una ciencia de la literatura*, trans. José Pérez Riesco, I (Madrid: Gredos,
1966), pp. 240–60; this work is applied to the *Lazarillo* prologue in 26, pp. 172–4.

ladas, y por ventura nunca oídas ni vistas", *Pr.* 1–2). Then comes
a subversive variant of the *topos* of "enseñar deleitando" (*Pr.* 3–5),[23]
which is followed by a passage of metaphors based on the "armas
y letras" *topos* (the combination of martial and literary excellence).
This passage (*Pr.* 17–26) contains three metaphors for the hazard-
ous activity of writing a book: the soldier attacking a besieged
town, the preacher, and the knight in a tournament. Thus the
metaphor from letters, which is more closely related to the subject
for comparison, is enclosed between two metaphors from arms.
The *Prólogo* contains one other *topos*, that of humility (*Pr.* 27–33),
and alludes to another, that of the book as ship. The dangers of sea
voyages in an age of oars and sail – which led to the secondary
meaning for "fortuna" of "a storm at sea" (p. 47, above) – made it
natural for authors to compare their temerity in launching their
works to that of the sailor facing the hazards of the ocean. The
final sentence of the *Prólogo* does not use this *topos* directly,[24] but
by claiming that Lazarillo's career shows the merit of those who,
"con fuerza y maña remando, salieron a buen puerto" (*Pr.* 39–40),
it links the life with the book, and brings the literary *topos* into
fresh contact with reality.

    Topoi are used in the narrative, though not as frequently as in
the *Prólogo*. The Blind Man is described, in allusion to the *topos*
of the greatest work of God, as the most astute person created by
God since the beginning of the world (1. 112–13); the claim to
divine sanction for the Blind Man's training of Lazarillo, hinted at
in the use of Biblical language in 1. 106–7, is thus implied more
strongly. The brevity *topos*, an assurance to the audience that they
would not be detained long, which was widely used in the centuries when amplification was the literary ideal, retained its use-
fulness during the few decades when brevity was the fashion:
"Mas por no ser prolijo dejo de contar muchas cosas" (1. 283; cf. 3.
322 and 501). This is linked on one occasion to the inexpressibility
topos, a way of stressing the magnitude and importance of the subject: "Y porque todos los que le veía hacer sería largo de contar,

---

[23] The verbs are not the expected "enseñe" and "deleite", but "agrade" and
"deleite", which are near-synonyms. See *20*, pp. 89–90.
[24] See Curtius, *European Literature*, pp. 128–30. Laurenti, *Los prólogos*, p. 63,
mistakenly claims a direct use.

diré uno" (5. 22–3). Another method of magnification is the out-doing *topos*, in which the subject is said to outdo some famous figure of antiquity in the very quality for which that figure is noted: "Pues en caso de medicina, decía que Galeno no supo la mitad que él para muela, desmayos, males de madre" (1. 123–4; cf. 3. 222–3).

Lazarillo, then, uses a wide variety of stylistic devices from a variety of sources.[25] They are seldom used for their own sake, and are seldom mechanical. Nearly always, they contribute to the book's humour, to its structure, to the expression of its themes. The same is true, as we shall now see, of the major aspect of style not so far covered: imagery.

[25] Some other stylistic features are discussed in *38*; *37*; *13*, pp. lxxi–lxxv; and *6*, pp. 38–44.

6 *Imagery*

Imagery is normally less frequent and less striking in narrative poetry than in the lyric, and even less frequent in prose fiction. *Lazarillo*, in this respect, conforms to expectations. Precise statistics are untrustworthy, since any two readers – or even the same reader on different days – will take different views of the boundary between image and literal statement. For what it is worth, however, we may note that this novel uses roughly 110 different images on some 175 occasions; this means, on average, one image for every ten lines of the Jones edition. Suspect though such attempts at precision must be, the figures do nevertheless provide some experimental support for the intuitive judgment that images are, in quantity, far from dominating *Lazarillo*'s style.

Neither are they qualitatively dominant: there is no image as fundamental as that of the journey in Jorge Manrique's *Coplas por la muerte de su padre*, or the dream in Calderón's *La vida es sueño*. Indeed, the author seems to neglect opportunities to establish a *Leitmotiv*: for example, given the nature of the picaresque novel, images of travel or of rising and falling might well occupy a commanding position. In *Lazarillo*, they are neither frequent nor insistent. However, they are, as we shall see, used to excellent effect. Rather than displaying his images prominently, the author subordinates them to his general plan; but within that plan he uses them economically, and often with subtlety and great effectiveness.

Two points about the distribution of images are of some interest. First, they are less frequent in the second half of the novel. No value can be attached to the figures for the very short *Tratados* IV and VI, but the other sections are probably long enough to give some meaning to the figures. The heavily literary *Prólogo* has on average one image every five lines, *Tratado* I every nine lines, and *Tratado* II every six, but in *Tratado* III the frequency falls to an average of one image every fourteen lines, and in *Tratado* V to every seventeen lines; in the final *Tratado* an image occurs every eleven lines on average. This is not the only feature which becomes scarcer as the book goes on : the first *tratado* is divided into numerous episodes, but the others are not. The author's technique seems to have evolved as he worked, in ways unaffected by any later polishing.

Secondly, there is some degree of image-bunching : once an image has been used, it may be used again very soon, or it may be quickly followed by the use of the same word in its literal sense, or by a related image. Thus, for example, of the nine metaphorical occurrences of "negro", six are found within two sections of roughly a hundred lines (1. 218, 326, 333; 3. 126, 208, 214), and in both of these groups the second and third occurrences are separated by only a few lines. Of the seven occurrences of devil images, five come within a 135-line section of *Tratado* I : "diablo", 1. 93; "endiablado", 1. 138, 152; "diablo", 1. 161; "demonio", 1. 228; and the same section includes a literal use of "diablo" (1. 190). In some cases, this bunching of images may be easily explained by the fact that they fit only one character, as when the Squire is compared to a greyhound (3. 311, 374). Even here, however, the images are closer together than one might expect in a 614-line *tratado*, and in most cases there is no such reason for restricting the image's use. There is, of course, nothing mysterious about this bunching : it arises from a normal psychological process of association, whose results may be either commonplace or memorable. In a literary masterpiece, they are likely to be memorable : for example, the two metaphorical uses of a closed door ("por cerrar la puerta a la sospecha", 2. 144–5, and "cierrase[1] la puerta a mi consuelo y la abriese a mis trabajos", 2. 204–5) refer to the contest of wits between Lazarillo and the Priest over the bread-chest, which ends with the exposure of Lazarillo's tricks and his eviction from the house : "Y santiguándose de mí como si yo estuviera endemoniado, tórnase a meter en casa y cierra su puerta" (2. 381–2). And so the *tratado* ends : metaphor has become painful reality.[2]

Of the areas from which images are drawn, religion is by far the most frequent : 19 different images are used 42 times, covering

---

[1] An imperfect subjunctive, not a reflexive present indicative, despite the diphthong. Of the most recent editions, *13* agrees with Jones, while *6*, *7* and *10* have "cerrase".

[2] There are also much less impressive uses of the same technique, e.g. the banal and mechanical use of a proverbial and a literal "puerta", 3. 548–50.

supernatural beings ("ángel", 2. 107, 127; "angélico", 2. 116; and the devil images mentioned above), the liturgy ("en dos credos", 2. 130), the next world ("paraíso", 2. 129), the mystical experience ("transportado en la divina esencia", 5. 123–4), the ecclesiastical hierarchy ("el Papa", 2. 43), sin and forgiveness ("pecador", 1. 304 and twelve other cases; "perdonar", 2. 272), and preaching ("predicar", *Pr.* 20). Animal images are next in popularity, but unlike the religious ones they are seldom repeated: only "galgo", "lobo" and "puerco" occur twice, while another 13 are each used on a single occasion. To the list of explicit images we should add the extended image which is implied when Lazarillo's depredations in the Priest's house are mistaken first for those of mice and then for those of a snake, a mistake which leads to his being treated as a snake (2. 329–36). Nearly all of the animals involved are domestic or otherwise familiar, and only "águila" (1. 113) and "ballena" (2. 353) are in any way exotic. A substantial group (10 images, 18 occurrences) comes from the field of illness and medicine, and several other areas are fairly well represented: warfare, chivalry and hunting (8 images, 9 occurrences); death (5 and 15); light, heat and cold (6 and 8); houses and contents (5 and 8); travel (5 and 8); cooking and eating (5 and 5). Other areas are – often surprisingly – comparatively neglected: money (3 and 4); domestic activities (3 and 3); sleep and waking (2 and 2). Clothing, landscape, law, sex and the weather are each represented by a single occurrence of a single image, and colour imagery is poor (one image, "negro", which occurs nine times).

To some extent the distribution of the different areas among the *tratados* is predictable. It is not surprising that more than half of the occurrences of religious images should be found in the two substantial *tratados* which deal with Lazarillo's life with the Priest and the Pardoner (17 and 5 occurrences respectively), or that animal images should be fairly evenly spread over the longer *tratados*, since they are not specifically associated with the way of life of any of the boy's masters; but it is surprising to find that two-thirds of the images from warfare, chivalry and hunting occur in *Tratado* II, and that, unless we include "galgo", none is in the seemingly appropriate *Tratado* III, in which Lazarillo is with a master whose life is, at least in theory, based on such activities. Yet this discrep-

ancy (unlike the near-total absence of financial imagery, which remains baffling) is probably only superficial. The story is being told
by the adult Lázaro, and if the imagery reflects his accumulated
experience, both direct and vicarious, there is no reason why images
derived from his expectations of life with the Squire should not be
absorbed along with the rest and used at will anywhere in the
work; the absence of such images from *Tratado* III may emphasize
the Squire's abdication of his traditional role.

The imagery of *Lazarillo* is predominantly urban, like the protagonist's life. The limitation of the action to town life, divorced
equally from court and countryside, has a precedent – and probably a direct inspiration – in *La Celestina*, though the imagery of
that work is both richer and more diverse. Lázaro's imaginative
range is – except for the prologue, which consciously and openly
draws on literary tradition – restricted to what he has seen and
heard, but there is of course no reason to suppose that the author
was similarly limited. It is much more likely that there was a
deliberate selection of image areas in the interests of psychological
realism.

Images in *Lazarillo* have two main functions: they underpin the
structure, and they play an important part in characterization (of
the narrator, as well as of those he describes). The links between
the beginning and end of the novel, the feeling that, although in
one sense Lázaro has made substantial worldly progress, in another
he has come full circle, are strengthened by such echoes as:

Mi viuda madre, como sin marido y sin abrigo se viese, determinó arrimarse a los buenos por ser uno dellos.   (1. 19–20)
Señor – le dije – yo determiné de arrimarme a los buenos.
(7.50)

Similarly, the decisive influence of the Blind Man's training and
example on the course of Lazarillo's life is emphasized by:

después de Dios éste me dio la vida, y siendo ciego me alumbró
y adestró en la carrera de vivir.   (1. 106–7)
Y pensando en qué modo de vivir haría mi asiento por tener
descanso y ganar algo para la vejez, quiso Dios alumbrarme y
ponerme en camino y manera provechosa.   (7.7–9)

The metaphorical "cornada" which the young Lazarillo receives

from the stone bull in Salamanca (1. 94) foreshadows the ending of
the novel, with the obvious (though never directly mentioned)
cuckold's horns which the mature Lázaro receives from the Archpriest. Moreover, the end of Lazarillo's time with the Blind Man
is related to its beginning through imagery as well as in other
ways: his head has been banged ("una gran calabazada", 1.93)
against the stone bull by his master, and now he causes the Blind
Man to dash his own head ("tan recio como si diera con una gran
calabaza", 1. 413–14) against a stone pillar, behind which the boy
stands "como quien espera tope de toro" (1. 406).

Both structural balance and characterization are served by the
images of enlightening and blinding in *Tratado* I. The Blind
Man's enlightenment of Lazarillo is referred to in the passage
quoted above. The dubious nature of that enlightenment (see the
end of Ch. 3) does not affect the issue: in the adult Lázaro's
view, the Blind Man has conferred a substantial benefit, but after
the blow with the wine-jar,

> en esto yo siempre le llevaba por los peores caminos, y adrede,
> por le hacer mal y daño: si había piedras, por ellas, si lodo, por
> lo más alto; que aunque yo no iba por lo más enjuto, hol-
> gábame a mí de quebrar un ojo por quebrar dos al que ninguno
> tenía.   (1. 233–7)

The Blind Man showed Lazarillo a profitable (metaphorical) path
through life, and is now repaid by being guided along the worst
(literal) roads; he shed metaphorical light for the boy, who now
makes his miserable existence still worse in ways summed up by
the proverbial – and, for a blind man, paradoxical – image of put-
ting both his eyes out. This image is echoed at the end of the
tratado, when religious sanction is claimed for the final and savage
trick which Lazarillo plays on his master:

> lo más principal, porque Dios le cegó aquella hora el entendi-
> miento (fue por darme dél venganza), creyóse de mí.   (1. 401–3)

Not only is the structure of the *tratado* made tighter and more
satisfying by these images, but we are given a mercilessly vivid
glimpse of Lazarillo's malice, since they link his cruelty to the

Blind Man not with the brutal treatment which provoked it, but with the benefits conferred and ungratefully received.[3]

Several of the animal images are important for characterization, though they lack the structural function of those just discussed. The first is used to dignify and exalt the Blind Man: "En su oficio era un águila" (1. 113). This reflects the medieval and Renaissance view of a universe in which hierarchical order was one of the fundamental principles, in which each order of creatures had its sovereign, and in which the eagle was generally regarded as the king of birds.[4] The Blind Man, then, is supreme among beggars as the eagle is among birds. There is humour in this, of course, because of the disproportion between the majesty of the eagle and the tattered squalor of the Blind Man. There is also paradox, for the eagle was famed for the sharpness of its sight;[5] the implication here is that blindness sharpened the wits, the inner eyes, of Lazarillo's first master. And there is also a point as wholly serious as anything can be in this subtle and ironic novel: the man who, we have just been told, "después de Dios . . . me dio la vida" (1. 106) is a master of his craft, and any lessons learned from him will, on his own level of worldly cunning, be effective.

The next animal image is also applied to the Blind Man, in the episode of the regurgitated sausage: "como debió sentir el huelgo, a uso de buen podenco" (1. 319–20). This begins a process of dehumanization, which is intensified when the Blind Man's nose is described as a "trompa" (1. 332), and continued when, in the episode of the stone pillar, he is compared to a bull (1. 406) and a goat (1. 411). This technique – the converse of the humanizing of animals, as in Aesop's Fables – was widely used in medieval literature and art, and the medieval tradition was inherited by the writers and artists of the Golden Age: Quevedo, for example, makes good use of it. The effect is to make the victim absurd, and

[3] We must again remember that the important point here is not what we, or the author, may think about these dubious benefits, but what the young Lazarillo and the mature Lázaro think. The latter regards them as benefits, and the cruelty as ungrateful, even if the former thought only of the provocation received.

[4] See E. M. W. Tillyard, *The Elizabethan World Picture* (London: Chatto and Windus, 1943), Ch. IV.

[5] See *The Book of Beasts*, trans. T. H. White (London: Cape, 1954), p. 105. The medieval bestiaries were still influential in the sixteenth century.

at the same time to demean him. The technique is used in other *tratados*. The Priest is compared to a wolf, in a particularly damaging context: "en cofradías y mortuorios que rezamos, a costa ajena comía como lobo" (2. 66–7). By traditional Christian metaphor a shepherd who should if necessary sacrifice his own life to protect his flock from the wolves, Lazarillo's second master himself becomes a wolf who devours the possessions of his sheep.

The Squire suffers more acutely from this technique of dehumanization. Comparison with a greyhound need not be unfavourable (Shakespeare makes Henry V praise his soldiers before Harfleur by saying "I see you stand like greyhounds in the slips"), but in *Lazarillo* it is: the Squire comes "a mediodía la calle abajo con estirado cuerpo, más largo que galgo de buena casta" (3. 373–5), the last three words being an ironic comment on his claim to be of good family; and the other simile makes the point even more clearly: "royendo cada huesecillo de aquéllos mejor que un galgo suyo lo hiciera" (3. 310–11). The picture of the unfortunate Squire eating like an animal does not depend solely on the greyhound simile; the beginning of the sentence whose end has just been quoted simply assumes that he is an animal. Lazarillo has acquired bread and a cow-heel, and when the starving Squire asks for some cow-heel, "Póngole en las uñas la otra" (3. 308). One animal is devoured by another.

Such images are double-edged. Whether we like it or not, we think less of the characters against whom they are used, but we also think less of the user. The joke about the Squire's "uñas" remains a joke, however uncomfortable we feel about it, but, as several critics have pointed out (e.g. *45*, pp. 49–50), this contemptuous jeering at a starving man forces us to realize the moral degradation of the joker. Yet some caution is necessary: the story is told, the joke made, by the adult Lázaro. We cannot assume that the child Lazarillo reacted to the situation in the same way, and we must therefore, while evaluating the narrator, be careful not to confuse him with the protagonist of years before.

The images in *Lazarillo* have other functions besides those discussed above; though less important, they are by no means negligible. One must suffice here by way of example: the use of "sangrar" to foreshadow scenes of violence. Although Lazarillo suffers

at the hands of almost all his masters (for the sufferings briefly
mentioned in the later *tratados*, see 4. 7–9, 5. 187 and 6. 2), and
although his hunger in the early days of serving the Squire is worse
than any he has known, he is the victim of physical brutality only
(as far as we can tell) in *Tratados* I and II. The Blind Man attacks
him savagely after the affair of the sausage (1. 336–40), and both
the episode of the wine-jar and that of the Priest's bread-chest end
with a blow to the head of such violence that Lazarillo needs pro-
longed patching-up (1. 208–20, 2. 334–41 and 352–8). Moreover,
Tratado I ends with such a severe injury to the Blind Man that
Lazarillo does not know whether or not it is fatal (2. 50–1). The
colouring given to the first two *tratados* by their near-monopoly of
images of illness and medicine (six in *Tratado* I, nine in II, and
only three in the rest of the novel) is therefore entirely appropriate.
These images are skilfully used: few of them are directly
associated with the bloodshed and brutality of the action, and their
use in other contexts heightens the impression of violence con-
taminating the whole of the two *tratados*. The most important
part is, however, played by the first two occurrences of such
images: "sangrías" (1. 11) and "sangraba" (1. 149), referring to
Lazarillo's father's thefts from the sacks of corn, and to Lazarillo's surreptitious opening of the Blind Man's bread-bag. We are
thus subconsciously prepared, by this metaphorical bloodletting,
for the real bloodshed which is to come. Furthermore, there is a
satisfying balance between image and reality, since the use of blood
imagery for corn and bread is far from arbitrary: these are lifeblood for Lazarillo, and without the desperate measures taken to
obtain them (by his father and then by himself) his life would be in
danger. But this metaphorical lifeblood must, it turns out, be paid
for with real blood.

7 Lázaro: narrator and protagonist

This short and apparently simple narrative proves to be remarkably mature, complex and subtle in its structure and its style. The same is true of the narrator's relation to his material and his audience. A fictional first-person narrative is common enough – it is normal in the picaresque novel, it occurs in several forms in medieval literature – but we expect to know who the narrator is. With very few exceptions, such narratives are either obviously fictional (often allegorical) adventures claimed by an author about whose life and other works we know a fair amount (Dante's *Divine Comedy* is one of the most famous examples of this class), or pseudo-autobiographies by an imaginary figure with the real author, who is known to us, looking over his shoulder. In both cases, it is relatively easy to distinguish, in Leo Spitzer's terms, between the poetic and the empirical I, between the person the author pretends to be and the person he really is.[1] In *Lazarillo de Tormes*, the supposedly empirical I, the narrator who explains himself and his work in the Prologue, is as much a fiction as the protagonist of his narrative, and the real author has covered his traces disconcertingly well.[2] What is more, the work is directed to an equally fictional audience, "Vuestra Merced", the friend of the Archpriest of San Salvador.

Several recent critics (notably Rico, *34*, pp. 277–87; *35*, pp. 21–5) have pointed out that "el caso", the squalid triangular relationship between Lázaro, his wife and the Archpriest, is at once the climax of the narration (it represents for Lázaro "la cumbre de toda buena fortuna") and its cause (Lázaro writes his story because Vuestra Merced has asked for a full account of "el caso"). This cause is not a mere formality: it was so unlikely that such a lowly character as

[1] Spitzer, "Note on the Poetic and the Empirical 'I' in Medieval Authors", *Traditio*, IV (1946), 414–22.

[2] A. Bell maintains that "the mantle of pseudo-autobiographer is not assumed until the second half of the prologue" ("The Rhetoric of Self-Defence of Lázaro de Tormes", *MLR*, LXVIII (1973), 84–93, at p. 84), but I am not convinced by his argument.

the town crier of Toledo would think his unremarkable life story
worth telling, or that anyone else would think it worth reading,
that even a fictional autobiography needed some such pretext in
order to convince its readers. There is, indeed, something implausible in the interest taken in Lázaro's life by the Archpriest's friend
and superior. For that reason – and despite the risks of speculating
about fictional characters outside the works in which they appear –
there is much to commend Richard Hitchcock's suggestion that
Lázaro has, self-importantly and absurdly, misunderstood, that
Vuestra Merced was interested in "el caso" only insofar as it
affected the Archpriest, and that the elaborate account of Lázaro's
early life is unnecessary.[3]

Whether or not we try to establish Vuestra Merced's reasons for
asking Lázaro for his account, it is obvious that the account is
aimed at self-justification, that Lázaro thinks it will illustrate a
general point (the self-made man is to be admired, *Pr.* 38–40), and
that it is to some extent suspect. The suspicion with which we view
it must go far beyond the realization that any autobiography is
inevitably biased. This is the story of a corruption, even if we do
not believe that Lazarillo is innocent when the narrative begins;
and the story is told by the corrupted man that he has become. He
is a liar and a hypocrite, he is anxious to make a favourable impression, and we know that even when still a child, he gave the Squire
a misleading account of himself. There is, then, no justification for
the view of many early critics of *Lazarillo*, that the protagonist is
an engaging rogue, that beneath the misdeeds forced on him by
society he has a heart of gold, and that we can automatically accept
the version of events that he chooses to give us. It is wrong to
equate the adult Lázaro with the child Lazarillo in his best
moments. However, the reaction against that error may have gone
too far. Woodward's article, which brought about a salutary reap-
praisal in several areas of *Lazarillo* studies, is implacably hostile not
only to the narrator but to the child who is the protagonist of the
first five *tratados*; the Lazarillo of *Tratado* III, who is generally
thought to show good qualities, is described as "a shifty wideboy"
and "this clever young thug" (*45*, pp. 49–50). This is, surely, the

---

[3] "Lazarillo and 'Vuestra Merced' ", *MLN*, LXXXVI (1971). 264–6.

mirror-image of the mistaken view mentioned above, since it still equates the narrator and the early protagonist.[4]

When we read *Lazarillo de Tormes*, our view is formed by :

1. the events,
2. the young Lazarillo's reactions to them,
3. the mature Lázaro's reflections on 1 and 2,
4. our reactions to 1, 2 and 3.

It is important to separate the first three elements, and not to transfer to any of them feelings and judgments that are appropriate only to another. If we allow our distaste for the hypocrisy and moral insensitivity of the mature Lázaro to colour our view of the young Lazarillo's actions and reactions, we fall into error. Yet, as Woodward points out, all our evidence is presented to us by the adult Lázaro. How far, then can we get behind these words and judge the events of the novel and the young Lazarillo's reactions?

It is generally agreed nowadays that we should not take everything in the novel at its face value, and that we should be especially sceptical when assured, in the Prologue and the last paragraph of the book, of Lázaro's final good fortune. The mature Lázaro is corrupt, so his criteria and judgments are corrupt too. But it is the mature Lázaro who is supposed to be telling the story, and therefore (insofar as the real author wants to disown Lázaro by making some of his style, and particularly his jokes and images, unpleasant) the corrupt style belongs to the mature and corrupted husband of the Archpriest's mistress. If this style makes us react unfavourably, as Woodward does to *Tratado* III, are we reacting to the behaviour of the young protagonist, or to the corrupt eyes through which we are forced to see it? How far, in general terms, is an adult's style a safe guide to the feelings of a child one or two decades before?

When Lázaro describes the starving Squire's hands as "las uñas", when he puns on "trabajo" and "lástima" (45, pp. 47–50), he is undoubtedly being witty at the expense of a suffering man. But we should not only remember that the wit is that of the adult looking back and reflecting, not that of the child reacting (all these

---

[4] Much of what follows is taken from my article ,"The Corrupted Vision : further thoughts on *LT*", *Forum for Modern Language Studies*, I (1965), 246–9.

specimens are part of the narrative, not of direct speech). We should also remember that verbal wit (in the twentieth-century, but not always in the seventeenth-century, sense) is one of the chief features of the style of *Lazarillo de Tormes*. Lázaro can be just as witty when writing about a master whom he openly recognizes as an enemy, the Blind Man: "holgábame a mí de quebrar un ojo por quebrar dos al que ninguno tenía" (1. 236–7), or when his own past physical suffering is involved (the blow from the "dulce y amargo jarro", 1. 198–211). The jokes in these two passages are of the same type as some of those used against the Squire. Thus it seems that we are here faced with a constant feature of the mature Lázaro's style, and that such a feature cannot be used with any confidence as a guide to the young Lazarillo's motives.

What, then, is the irreducible minimum on which we can base our judgments? The answer is, I suggest, the overt factual narrative. It seems to be a well-established convention that however sceptical readers may be about a character's professed motives, the actions of the characters and the physical facts of the situation are to be accepted as the narrator states them unless the reader is specifically warned to the contrary. This convention is generally accepted even today, when novelists are, with some justice, more widely suspected of playing tricks on their readers than were their sixteenth-century predecessors; even the apparently fundamental ambiguity that has distressed critics of *The Turn of the Screw* may not have been intended by the author.[5] If modern novelists, whatever their commitment to ambiguity in some directions, need to tell us when their narrative is not to be trusted,[6] it is fair to assume that the sixteenth-century reader, less accustomed than we are to obscurity in novels, could take the facts of *Lazarillo de Tormes* to be facts. When, in a somewhat less trusting age than the 1550s, Cervantes described Don Quijote's madness, he very carefully explained the difference between what the knight thought he was doing and what he was in fact doing; for example:

[5] See Wayne C. Booth, *The Rhetoric of Fiction* (Chicago: Univ. Press, 1961), pp. 311–15. Booth goes on to discuss other cases of ambiguity in the modern novel, but these are generally questions of motive and interpretation, not of factual narrative. His remarks on "Troubles with irony in earlier literature" (pp. 316–23) are of considerable interest for *Lazarillo*.

[6] I deal with this question in greater detail on p. 248 of my article (see note 4, above).

En esto, descubrieron treinta o cuarenta molinos de viento que hay en aquel campo, y así como don Quijote los vio, dijo a su escudero: – La ventura va guiando nuestras cosas mejor de lo que acertáramos a desear, porque ves allí, amigo Sancho Panza, donde se descubren treinta, o pocos más, desaforados gigantes . . . (*Don Quijote* I. viii)

Not until we come to Quevedo's *Sueños* and Gracián's *Criticón* is there any question of objective reality dissolving in subjective illusion, and here the allegorical, "non-photographic" nature of the work is clear from the start (see p. 56, above).

Therefore, since there is no warning from the author of *Lazarillo de Tormes*, we must recognize that the actions described by Lázaro did in fact occur. Indeed, if we refuse to recognize this, we are left knowing nothing of what happens in the book, and are unable to formulate any critical opinions – this sobering reflection is, of course, hinted at by Woodward (p. 44).

Lazarillo, then, really did have his head banged on the stone bull by the Blind Man; he really did get his revenge by causing the Blind Man to jump at full speed into a post; and he really did feed his third master until that master deserted him without a word. "Clearly", as Woodward says (p. 47), "the action of a servant in feeding his starving master is a Christian action." If we are to see the Lazarillo of *Tratado* III as no more sympathetic a character than the adult Lázaro of *Tratado* VII, this Christian action must somehow be devalued. I have already argued that the style in which it is narrated cannot be the basis of such a devaluation, since this style belongs to the narrator, long since corrupted; what indications we have of the narrative style employed by the younger protagonist suggest that it was rather different (e.g. 3. 194–209 and 257–9). Are there any other actions that outweigh this Christian one? Did Lazarillo bring food into the house without giving some to his master? If he did, we know nothing of it. Did he refrain from bringing in food when he could have done so? It would seem that he did not. Admittedly, he received some food from the women next door, but very little, since they themselves did not have much: "de la laceria que les traían me daban alguna cosilla, con la cual muy pasado me pasaba" (3. 368–9). Did Lazarillo – and this is, I think, the last possibility of devaluing his charitable action in feeding the Squire – torment him deliberately and un-

necessarily? Woodward (pp. 48–50) and Lomax (*28*, p. 372) believe
that he did. Yet Lazarillo is dealing here with a man of obsessive
pride, a man whose concern for his reputation has become a full-
time job, almost a monomania. It is not always easy, or even safe,
to rush in with offers of help in such cases. Is it really surprising or
reprehensible that Lazarillo had to lure his master into eating?

If we revert to the traditional idea of Lazarillo's actions in
Tratado III as charitable ones, it becomes easier to plot the course
of his corruption. Two traumatic experiences mark the stages of
this corruption: the well-known episode of the bull of Salamanca,
and the less widely remarked shock of the Squire's desertion, "do
acabé de conocer mi ruin dicha". This is, of course, the adult Lázaro
speaking again, but his words make sense, since Lazarillo has this
time been betrayed not by the Blind Man, a stranger who quickly
becomes an enemy, but by the starving man whom he has fed.
Henceforward he can trust nobody. And nobody can trust him –
as servant, husband, friend, or as interpreter of the story.[7]

There is, then, some difficulty in discovering the young Lazarillo's immediate reactions to the events of *Tratados* I–V, since we
cannot trust the adult Lázaro's report of his younger self's feelings,
but some help is available from the asides which are given in direct
speech (see *10*, p. 30; *18*). These, like the overt factual narrative,
should on the whole be taken as an authentic record. They may
occasionally seem too mature for a child of that age, as when the
eight-year-old Lazarillo exclaims "¡Cuántos debe de haber en el
mundo que huyen de otros porque no se veen a sí mesmos!" (*1*.
42–3), but even in such cases the style differs from that of the adult
narrator.[8] These asides differ also from those found in some other
works. As Carey shows (*18*, p. 123), they are not overheard by any
other character, and therefore have no influence on the action.
Secondly, although those that are ironic or sarcastic in tone out-
number those that are merely reflective (*18*, p. 131), none of them
shows duplicity, whereas in *La Celestina* this is one of the main

---

[7] Gilman argues, probably correctly, that Lázaro's full degradation comes only
with his decision to tell his story (*22*, p. 154), and he makes interesting comments
on the adult Lázaro's style.

[8] Carey rightly distinguishes them from Lázaro's direct addresses to the reader,
whereas even such shrewd critics as Durand (*20*, p. 94) and Woodward (*45*, p. 46)
fall into the trap of identifying the two groups.

functions of the aside. This does not, of course, mean that Lazarillo is incapable of duplicity, merely that his reactions to the events are relatively fresh and can be accepted as a guide to what he was like as a child.

Just as the asides represent the child, so the Prologue and the end of *Tratado* VII show us the adult in his final phase (final as far as we are concerned, that is). These two sections balance each other in the novel's structure, as we saw in Chapter 4, but they also do this in a more subtle and fundamental way. *Tratado* VII is the point in the narrative at which the protagonist merges with the narrator, and the present tense (not merely the historic present) becomes appropriate.[9] There is, however, a disconcerting variation in the use of tenses. Lázaro's enjoyment of his "oficio real", of his new-found prosperity, and of his married life – all of this on a squalid level, all of it under the ambiguous patronage of the Archpriest, but all of it representing solid achievement for the child of the Salamanca slums – is normally described in the present:

> vivo y resido (7. 13–14) . . . tengo cargo de pregonar los vinos (15) . . . casi todas las cosas al oficio tocantes pasan por mi mano (20) . . . tengo en mi señor acipreste todo favor y ayuda (31–2) . . .

So are the neighbours' gossip and Lázaro's reaction to it:

> hasta agora no estoy arrepentido (30) . . . malas lenguas . . . no nos dejan vivir (37–8) . . . cuando alguno siento que quiere decir algo della, le atajo y le digo (66–7) . . . Desta manera no me dicen nada, y yo tengo paz en mi casa. (76)

This seems clear enough, but three verbs contradict it.

> Los domingos y fiestas casi todas las comíamos en su casa [i.e. the Archpriest's house] (35–6) . . . Esto fue el mesmo año que nuestro victorioso Emperador en esta insigne ciudad de Toledo entró y tuvo en ella cortes (77–8) . . . Pues en este tiempo estaba en mi prosperidad y en la cumbre de toda buena fortuna. (80–1)

The clear implication (clear once Woodward pointed it out, *45*, pp. 50–1, though previous critics had missed it) is that, although

---

[9] There are occasional references to present circumstances at earlier points, e.g. 1. 211 and 3. 343; see *34*, pp. 282–3. Dr Halkhoree reminds me that a similar merging of narrator and protagonist occurs at the end of *Guzmán de Alfarache*.

Lázaro still has the post of *p 'egonero*, still has enough to eat, is still married, and can still hold the gossipers at bay, the best times are over. The cordiality of his relationship with the Archpriest has cooled, and the descent from the top of Fortune's wheel has begun (which, to any reader of that time, must have carried the further implication of an inevitable and ever-accelerating descent to final disaster). Rico suggests (*35*, pp. 22–3) that "fue" and "estaba" are merely "un cultismo sintáctico, con un calco del 'pasado epistolar' común en latín", by which the writer of a letter recognizes that what is present to him will be past to the recipient; but, as Bell says, this raises fresh problems.[10] Why should only a few verbs be in the past, when many others are in the present? Why should the "pasado epistolar" imply the passage of years rather than days ("Esto fue el mesmo año")? The distribution of past and present tenses is logical if one assumes that things have begun to go wrong in the *ménage à trois*, and it matches the image of Fortune's wheel. The enquiries made by Vuestra Merced may even be one of the worries that Lázaro now has to face.

There is an equally thought-provoking, and until recently equally neglected, discrepancy in the Prologue. Like the book as a whole, the Prologue is addressed to Vuestra Merced; it introduces the explanation asked for, and offered to, one influential person. This is clear enough in the second half of the Prologue, with its humility *topos* (*Pr.* 27–33) and its direct reference to Vuestra Merced's request, but it is not easy to reconcile with the first half, which refers to a wide audience (*Pr.* 37 echoes this), speaks of literary fame (14–16), and even says that "muy pocos escribirían para uno solo" (13–14). Yet such reconciliation is possible: Durand suggests that "what might have started out as an account for one man has reached more ambitious and pretentious proportions" (*20*, p. 91; cf. *26*, p. 173). Lázaro has, at least on the surface, an almost limitless capacity for being pleased with himself, even in circumstances that most people would regard as unenviable (a despised job, cuckoldry). This does not exclude the possibility that, as Truman argues, Lázaro to some extent takes an ironic view of himself and of his achievement (*40*; *41*; *42*) – we have already seen that

---

[10] "The Rhetoric of Self-Defence" (see note 2, above), p. 86.

his sardonic humour is applied to his own misfortunes as well as to those of others. As Truman says,

> at one and the same time, he does and does not take himself and his achievement seriously. He comes before us as one who feels he has made substantial material progress in life and yet is so far conscious of the limited nature of what he has achieved that he enjoys the comedy of pretending to have achieved more than he has in fact done. (*40*, p. 605)

What more natural – especially in one who congratulates himself on being able to see the irony of his situation – than that dreams of a new career as a distinguished writer should take hold of him, that literary fame should be the new "buen puerto" towards which he rows (*Pr.* 39–40)? Here, as with Vuestra Merced's reasons for asking about "el caso", there is a danger of speculating too hard about the real lives of fictional characters, but it is worth remembering that (as we saw at the end of Ch. 6) the launching of a ship on perilous seas was at this period a frequent image for the publication of a book (hence the frontispiece to *La pícara Justina*).

The desire for fame as a spur to literary creation is substantiated by a quotation from Cicero: "a este propósito dice Tulio: La honra cría las artes" (*Pr.* 16–17). *Honos alit artes*, yet (*34*, p. 282) this work of art grows out of dishonour, since the scandal of "el caso" led Vuestra Merced to make the enquiries to which Lázaro's narrative is a reply.

This brings us back to the relationship between the Prologue and the end of *Tratado* VII. The first part of VII shows Lázaro only as protagonist, the second part as protagonist and narrator simultaneously, thus leading into the first part of the Prologue, where he is merely an author. Guillén and Lázaro Carreter suggest that the Prologue may be regarded as a final chapter (*10*, p. 10; *26*, p. 173). In the second part of the Prologue, while still primarily a narrator, he is also the protagonist, the central figure of "el caso", and this section is immediately followed by *Tratado* I, in which Lazarillo appears only as protagonist, a role which he will keep until near the end of *Tratado* VII. Thus the book becomes cyclical. The close connection between the end of *Tratado* VII and the beginning of the Prologue is stressed by two further parallels: Lázaro addresses and challenges his neighbours about his marriage (7. 68–75), just

as he addresses (and challenges?) a wider audience about his book
(*Pr.* 1–26), though in both cases he knows he is on dangerous
ground; and the reference to the splendour of the Emperor's entry
into Toledo (7. 77–9) matches the erudition and display of the
topoi and the literary references in the first paragraph of the Prologue.

Lázaro's life in Toledo with the Archpriest's mistress is uncomfortably similar to his life as a child on the banks of the Tormes,
though at a higher economic level. In Woodward's phrase, "his
end is in his beginning" (45, p. 45). The same can be said of the
novel, as we saw at the beginning of this chapter: "el caso" is both
the cause and the climax of the story. Lázaro's life and the story
which tells about it are, looked at in one light, both cyclical, though
with the form of a spiral rather than a mere circle: Lázaro does
rise economically, the story does reach a point where (in terms of
narrative skill) it can be introduced with flourishes usually reserved
for more elevated subjects. And just as Lázaro's wife merges into
his mother,[11] and "el caso" into the creative process of the novel, so
Lázaro the protagonist is at once distinct from and merged with
Lázaro the narrator, and with the narrative itself. Life and story
are one.

---

[11] This is true structurally and thematically; Gilman, having raised the question
of the Oedipus myth (22, p. 162), is right to dismiss it.

A detailed study of *Lazarillo*'s sources would be inappropriate to this series of Critical Guides, and in any case I have little to add to the work that has already been done. It is, however, necessary to consider the way in which the author uses the popular and literary material available to him.

Lazarillo de Tormes draws on traditional popular material at both the narrative and the verbal level; that is to say, it incorporates folktales and proverbs (Bataillon reminds us, *16*, pp. 33–4, that the division between these genres may not be watertight). It is certain that a contest of wits between a blind man and his boy was a subject for folk humour in the Middle Ages (they appear in a French play and in a drawing in the margin of a manuscript; for details of these and other points, see Jones, *12*, pp. xvii–xxiv). Some scholars would take the matter further, attach the name Lazarillo to the boy, and/or make the Squire into a similarly folkloric figure,[1] but this is probably mistaken. Rather than being a folkloric figure borrowed by the author, he is the author's imaginative creation who incorporates some folkloric aspects; the distinction is important.

Many narrative elements in *Lazarillo* may be identified as folk-motifs, as Lida de Malkiel and Lázaro Carreter have shown (*27*; *26*): for example, the bull of Salamanca, the hero of humble and mysterious origins, the trickster's escape from his creditors, and the misunderstanding over the "casa lóbrega y obscura". All of these are used to enhance the comedy of the work, the second by parody and the others directly. Moreover, the first has both a structural and a thematic function; the third is structurally important; and the fourth emphasizes a theme. These cases are fairly typical

[1] Angel González Palencia, *Del Lazarillo a Quevedo: estudios histórico-literarios, cuarta serie* (Madrid: CSIC, 1946), pp. 10–15; and Bataillon, *16*, pp. 27–45. C. A. Jones sees the novel as a compilation of traditional material, "*LT*: survival or precursor?", in *Litterae hispanae et lusitanae*, ed. Hans Flasche (München: Hueber, 1968), pp. 181–8. Lázaro Carreter's excellent discussion of folklore in *Lazarillo* is marred only by his insistence that the Squire is incipiently folkloric (*26*, pp. 134–43), which blurs the useful distinctions he establishes elsewhere.

of the author's skill in making his material serve more than one purpose. The episode of the "casa lóbrega y obscura" illustrates the difficulty of deciding whether some elements are folkloric: a manuscript collection of stories contains a very similar joke, but it is impossible to tell whether this or *Lazarillo* came first (*12*, p. xxi), and the question has been resolved only recently, with the discovery of the story in a medieval Arabic work which makes it clear that this is indeed a traditional tale.[2] It is also possible for folklore influences to show themselves in the structure of a work, independently of the use of folk-motifs for the content, and this seems to have happened to some extent in *Lazarillo,* although most of the structure is to be accounted for differently (see Ch. 4, above).

It is hard to decide where the author obtained his folkloric material. Some of it may well have come from literary sources such as collections of *exempla* (see Ch. 4, note 5), some from oral tradition. There is not, in pre-*Lazarillo* Spain, a tradition of jest-books comparable to the German *Till Eulenspiegel* (compiled about 1500),[3] but none is needed to account for the folklore in this novel; and, whatever the range of sources available to the author, the most significant factor is the way in which he transformed the material, weaving it into a more complex structure, taking a close interest in the characters (Lida de Malkiel points out, *27*, p. 351, that folktales generally pay little attention to character), and en-dowing it with thematic importance. That being said, we must of course keep firmly in mind that what attracted the author to such material in the first place was presumably its humour, and that a major reason for its presence in the novel is that it makes readers laugh.

Proverbs play a less important, but far from negligible, part in *Lazarillo,* and recent editors have drawn attention to them in footnotes. They serve two purposes: first, they lend a vivid and natural tone to the narrative and the conversation; and secondly,

---

[2] *15*, pp. 57–65. For comments on this episode see, in addition to works listed in the Bibliographical Note, Marcel Bataillon, *Défense et illustration du sens littéral* (Modern Humanities Research Association Presidential Address, 1967), pp. 18–20.

[3] Bataillon (*16*, p. 35) suggests that *Lazarillo* borrows some material either from the German text or from a French translation. For the post-*Lazarillo* period, see Maxime Chevalier, *Cuentecillos tradicionales en la España del Siglo de Oro* (Bordeaux: Institut d'Etudes Ibériques et Ibéro-Américaines, 1971).

they sometimes contribute to the irony of the book by the context in which they are set, as with "arrimarse a los buenos por ser uno dellos" (1. 20).

There is inevitably some overlap between popular and literary material; the transmission of folktales by literary texts has already been mentioned, and what some critics regard as a conscious and substantial literary borrowing from the fifteenth-century Italian writer Masuccio Salernitano, the episode of the Pardoner, is thought by others to be of popular origin (see *12*, p. xx). A different kind of overlap is represented by the ballads, popular poetry which became fashionable among cultivated people and was set to music and sometimes recast by court musicians. A reminiscence of two ballads is used to satirize the pretensions of the Squire:

> Y súbese por la calle arriba con tan gentil semblante y continente, que quien no le conociera pensara ser muy cercano pariente al conde de Arcos, o a lo menos camarero que le daba de vestir.
> (3. 190–3; see *10*, pp. 157–8)

The author's use of literary sources has been much discussed, and some suggestions have met with little support: for instance, H. R. Jauss's belief that the autobiographical form of the novel is a parodic echo of St Augustine's *Confessions*[4] is not shared by those who have considered the question more recently. The probable or certain sources which have been established are, however, enough to show that the author was a man of fairly wide reading who had the culture and the self-confidence to adapt what he read to his own purposes. His use of the Bible was discussed in Ch. 3. Among secular writers, some provide a single but important quotation (Cicero's "La honra cría las artes", *Pr.* 17; Blanquat suggests a more substantial debt to Cicero, *17*, p. 50), others a possible reminiscence (Dante and the doorway of the Squire's house; see p. 42, above).

There is one explicit allusion to the Castilian love poetry of the preceding century, when Lázaro describes the Squire's encounter with the local prostitutes: "él estaba entre ellas hecho un Macías, diciéndoles más dulzuras que Ovidio escribió" (3. 222–3). Classical

[4] "Ursprung und Bedeutung der Ich-Form im *LT*", *Romanistisches Jahrbuch*, VIII (1957), 290–311.

and medieval poetry are thus invoked to heighten the description, and of course to heighten the comedy, since the elaborately sighing lover will be unable to pay, and the girls "dejáronle para el que era" (3. 230). These names do not prove familiarity with either classical or *cancionero* poetry: they were commonplaces of the time, and the name of Macías exemplified the suffering lover to many who had never read his poems. The remainder of this passage shows, however, that the author knew *cancionero* poetry rather well. The Squire's symptoms of passion – "tomóle tal calofrío que le robó la color del gesto, y comenzó a turbarse en la plática" (3. 226–8) – are standard in the courtly poetry, and in the prose romances, of that period, though here they come from a hilariously uncourtly cause: the girls have offered their services, but the Squire is "tan frío de bolsa cuanto estaba caliente del estómago" (3. 226). The conflict between passion and chastity was familiar enough in literature (perhaps the best known example for early readers of *Lazarillo* was Garcilaso's sonnet "En tanto que de rosa y d'azucena"), but lust foiled by bankruptcy was a literary novelty. And the debt to poetic convention (and therefore the joke) extends further. Lázaro begins his report of the incident thus:

> en una huerta vi a mi amo en gran recuesta con dos rebozadas mujeres, al parecer de las que en aquel lugar no hacen falta, antes muchas tienen por estilo de irse a las mañanicas del verano a refrescar y almorzar sin llevar qué por aquellas frescas riberas, con confianza que no ha de faltar quién se lo dé. (3. 215–20)

This is the convention of the *alborada*, or poem of dawn meeting; the hour, the season (spring or early summer), the place (the river banks), the desire are there, but the characters are out of place. The Squire and the poetic conventions of the time are simultaneously displayed for our amusement.

It is possible that the author also makes use of those conventions to describe Lazarillo's longing for food and wine (1. 180, 203, 216, 297–8; 2. 151–2). *Cancionero* poetry was full of paradoxical antithesis and of images of death (Garcilaso had broken away from this convention, but the *Cancionero general*, the great collection of fifteenth-century poetry, was only just falling from favour when *Lazarillo* was composed, and it was even reprinted with additions as late as 1557). In these cases the echo is distant and muted, but the Squire's *alborada* leaves no room for doubt.

Spanish prose literature of the preceding decades also, and hardly surprisingly, left its mark on *Lazarillo*. The parody of the Beatitudes in *Tratados* I and VII is probably taken from *La Celestina*, and the debt does not end there: there are other apparent reminiscences, and the use of memory as a structural device seems to owe something to the earlier work.[5] Beyond that, there is the wider question of *La Celestina*'s influence on all sixteenth-century Spanish depictions of low life. Prose fiction of a very different kind, the chivalresque romance, is a principal object of parody at the beginning of *Lazarillo*, and this parody is resumed at intervals throughout the book.

The autobiographical form of the novel also has literary precedents. As Bataillon shows, fictional first-person narrative was in vogue in the 1550s (*16*, p. 50), and this almost certainly affected the author's choice of form. It seems clear, however, that the dominant influence is that of *The Golden Ass* and especially, despite the arguments of Jean Molino, the pseudo-Lucian version of that work.[6] This model may well have been supplemented by the formal letters which also flourished in the first half of the sixteenth century, and some of which, especially those from the New World, related the success of men from relatively humble backgrounds (*26*, pp. 41–6; *35*, pp. 15–21). And a final contributory factor may have been the stock speech of self-justification uttered by a self-made man in many Renaissance treatises on true nobility, though in this case the relation between *Lazarillo* and supposed source would be parodic (*42*, p. 45).

This brings us to what may best be termed a thematic source. The moral of the novel as claimed by Lázaro himself is that:

> consideren los que heredaron nobles estados cuán poco se les debe, pues fortuna fue con ellos parcial, y cuánto más hicieron los que, siéndoles contraria, con fuerza y maña remando, salieron a buen puerto.   (*Pr.* 37–40)

This is echoed after the incident of the bull of Salamanca:

[5] Dorothy S. Severin, *Memory in La Celestina* (London: Tamesis, 1970), pp. 67–9.

[6] Molino, "*LT* et les *Métamorphoses* d'Apulée", *Bulletin Hispanique*, LXVII (1965), 322–33. Lázaro Carreter has demonstrated the debt to pseudo-Lucian (see p. 35, above).

Huelgo de contar a V.M. estas niñerías para mostrar cuánta
virtud sea saber los hombres subir siendo bajos, y dejarse bajar
siendo altos cuánto vicio.   (1. 108–10)

The assertion that true nobility consists not in high rank and inherited wealth but in virtue, intelligence and effort seems platitu-
dinous today, but in the Renaissance it was a hotly debated issue.
Many treatises maintained this view, while a large body of traditional opinion held that that social mobility offended against the
divinely established order. Praise of the "homo novus", the virtuous self-made man, goes back to Seneca and Boethius, is revived
by Dante and Petrarch, and is widespread in the fifteenth and sixteenth centuries. Lázaro's words can be matched time after time
in the treatises, though this fact escaped notice until recently.[7]
There can be no doubt that what Lázaro says is fully and consciously within the "homo novus" tradition. Two questions now
arise: does *Lazarillo* draw on any specific works, or is this a
general indebtedness? And how does Lázaro's career exemplify
his theoretical statement? An answer to the first question has been
tentatively given by Truman, who suggests Seneca's Epistle XLIV,
the opening dialogues of Petrarch's *De remediis adversae fortunae*,
and Erasmus's *Praise of Folly* as sources (42). The similarities are
interesting but, as Truman recognizes, not conclusive.[8] As to the
second, Lázaro's career in some ways meets the requirements of
the treatises – he starts under grave disadvantages, he displays
energy and ingenuity, he betters himself economically, and he ends
with a post in the public service – but in other ways he falls far
short of the "homo novus". His post of *pregonero* is disreputable,
he takes on some of the qualities of the Squire, who is a good
example of the well-born and decadent failure, and, most important of all, he lacks virtue. *Lazarillo de Tormes* is, then, a parody
of the "homo novus" tradition, and this seems to be one of the most
important of its parodies.

The novel's literary debts thus range from the borrowing of a

[7] The discovery was made almost simultaneously by Lázaro Carreter (*26*,
pp. 178–83), Rico (*13*, p. 14; *35*, pp. 46–9), and, in much greater detail, Truman
(*41*); see also *17*, pp. 48–50.

[8] Another debt to Erasmus is suggested but, again, not proved, by Ann Wiltrout,
"The *LT* and Erasmus' *Opulentia sordida*", *Romanische Forschungen*, LXXXI
(1969) 550–64.

single sentence, through a generalized awareness of a group of poetic conventions, to the adoption of a structure or (parodically) a major theme. These, and folklore material, are incorporated for equally varied reasons: to add decoration, provide anecdotes, increase the novel's irony, strengthen its structure, or emphasize a theme.

Despite its brevity, *Lazarillo de Tormes* combines a number of major themes, whose relative importance changes as the novel progresses, which are interwoven, and which are almost all announced in the Prologue and the first third of *Tratado* I.

One of the most important is firmly stated at the end of the Prologue:

> consideren los que heredaron nobles estados cuán poco se les debe, pues fortuna fue con ellos parcial, y cuánto más hicieron los que, siéndoles contraria, con fuerza y maña remando, salieron a buen puerto.   (*Pr.* 37–40)

As we have just seen, this expresses the doctrine that the virtuous self-made man is truly noble, and one may query its intellectual consistency in the light of what actually happens in the book (Woodward takes an extreme position, describing it as "persuasive but silly claptrap", *45*, p. 46). We must now consider it as a statement of theme, an assertion that the book will be about success and failure, rise and fall, and as such it proves accurate. Lázaro's career is a succession of minor rises and falls, but in economic terms, measured by the simple test of whether he has enough to eat, it declines to the middle of *Tratado* III (not the end, since he is from time to time able to feed his master as well as himself), and then begins to rise (e.g. "Este fue el primer escalón que yo subí para venir a alcanzar buena vida", 6. 6–7), reaching "la cumbre de toda buena fortuna" (7. 80–1). Yet this rise, modest though it is, is dearly bought, and the Prologue hints at the price: "con fuerza y maña" (*Pr.* 39) – not virtue, but strength and skill (or, less charitably interpreted, force and cunning). The economic rise is a moral fall (*44*, p. 278; and the case is fully argued by Wardropper, *43*). Or, in terms of the name which the author chose for his protagonist, Lazarus becomes Dives morally as well as economically (see the end of Ch. 3).

The theme of Fortune, which obsessed men of the late Middle Ages and the Renaissance,[1] is linked with that of rise and fall both at the end of the Prologue and at the end of *Tratado* VII. There is an important difference between these two passages, since the first suggests that Fortune, who smiles on the high-born, is to the "homo novus" Lázaro an enemy who must be overcome, while the second shows her as favouring Lázaro. Between these passages, Fortune is hostile (1. 44; 2. 196–8; 3. 76, 354, 400–1, and 536 – the last of these applies to the Squire), and "desastre" is used as a synonym for "fortuna" (3. 326). The title of the novel is therefore ambiguous: are the words "fortunas y adversidades" synonyms, or do they form a contrasting pair? The answer depends partly on whether one connects them with the main body of Fortune references or with 7.81, and partly on whether one regards the title as having been chosen by Lázaro or by the real author. But the final interpretation should be pessimistic, in accordance with the implications of decline in the novel's final sentence.

Fortune, like the closely associated theme of rise and fall, is important throughout the novel. Poverty and hardship, chiefly expressed in terms of hunger, dominate the first three *tratados* and then fade away. Hunger is not mentioned in the description of Lazarillo's life with his parents, but it occurs in an extreme form ("tanto que me mataba a mí de hambre", 1. 133) soon after he begins to work for the Blind Man. Thereafter it occupies Lazarillo, often to the exclusion of everything else, and Tarr shows (*39*, p. 410) how it rises to a climax during *Tratados* I–III.[2] After that, the quest for security, status and a modest level of prosperity replaces the desperate struggle for food. That struggle is, in *Tratados* I and II, a contest of wits between Lazarillo and his masters, and several times it erupts into physical violence ("con fuerza y maña"). In *Tratado* II the contest ends as soon as the Priest discovers what has been happening, but the Blind Man keeps Lazarillo on after he has been found out several times. Is this merely because it was difficult for him to find a replacement, or does he welcome the battle of wits? Is the bull episode a challenge as well as an initiation?

During these *tratados*, hypocrisy plays a considerable part,

---

[1] Howard R. Patch, *The Goddess Fortuna in Mediaeval Literature* (Cambridge, Mass.: Harvard Univ. Press, 1927), gives abundant examples from literature and art. See *19*, pp. 275–6, for this theme in *Lazarillo*.

[2] It is supplemented by exposure and the need for shelter: see *22*, p. 161.

though it does not become dominant until later. The first conscious hypocrite is the Blind Man:

> En su oficio era un águila; ciento y tantas oraciones sabía de coro: un tono bajo, reposado y muy sonable que hacía resonar la iglesia donde rezaba, un rostro humilde y devoto que con muy buen continente ponía cuando rezaba.   (1. 113–16)

Yet "jamás tan avariento ni mezquino hombre no vi" (1. 132–3), and when those who paid him to pray departed, the prayers ceased at once (1. 165–6). The story of Lazarillo's black half-brother running in fear from his black father and crying "¡Madre, coco!" (1. 36–9) prepares us for this and for subsequent developments, since what the child genuinely does not see in himself, other characters in the novel deliberately choose not to see. Hypocrisy reaches a peak with the Priest of Maqueda, who labels his own blatant avarice and gluttony as generosity and temperance, but perhaps he is too blatant to be a really accomplished hypocrite. It recedes in *Tratado* III, though not for reasons that do much credit to the Squire, since the gap between what he seems to be and what he is on the social and economic level is at least as wide as it is on the moral level with other characters. Moreover, his ambition is to be the hypocritical adviser of a great lord (3. 515–30). Incompetence rather than virtue seems to stand between him and the depths of hypocrisy, and the part that he might have played is to some extent taken over by Lazarillo (3. 57–8, 82, 116, 240–1, and 280). The growth of hypocrisy, having faltered a little in *Tratado* III, is strongly resumed in IV (the Friar), and above all in V (the Pardoner), reaching its true climax in *Tratado* VII, where Lázaro and the Archpriest are in tacit agreement, a conspiracy of hypocrisy, to deny the true nature of Lázaro's marriage.

Various subsidiary themes are associated with hypocrisy. Betrayal makes an early appearance, when the child Lazarillo is interrogated about the activities of his mother and Zaide:

> a mí con amenazas me preguntaban, y como niño respondía, y descubría cuanto sabía con miedo, hasta ciertas herraduras que por mandado de mi madre a un herrero vendí.   (1. 54–7)

It is one of the ironies of the book that naivety and fear should lead

Lazarillo to betray his mother before his corruption by his masters begins.

Illusions of various kinds also begin early: Lazarillo's transformation of coins from *blancas* into *medias blancas* (1. 153–63; for further examples, see p. 55, above). The Squire succeeds in halfconvincing himself that fantasy has become reality: he urges on Lazarillo the need to take precautions against thieves when the boy has already discovered that there is nothing in the house to steal (3. 140 and 188). Illusion, however, differs from hypocrisy, in that reality generally breaks it down: Lazarillo's substitutions and disguises in *Tratados* I and II are brutally and painfully revealed, and the Squire has in the end to admit the emptiness of his house (3. 271–7 and 392–5). Only on the linguistic and moral levels is illusion maintained: the Pardoner's pseudo-Latin convinces his audience (5. 18–19), and on the moral level hypocrisy is still in tenuous control at the end of the novel.

The misdeeds of the clergy are not limited to hypocrisy, but it is an essential element in all of them. The theme of clerical vice is not developed until *Tratado* II, and does not dominate the book until *Tratado* IV, but it is announced in Lazarillo's already-quoted observation about Zaide's thefts (1. 50–4).

Finally, there is the theme of honour, one aspect of which is outlined in the Prologue: "La honra cría las artes" (*Pr.* 17), and the succeeding lines show that honour here means fame, public esteem. Little is heard of any aspect until *Tratado* III, where it becomes a major theme. The Squire's obsessive concern with rank, cleanliness and all the outer trappings of public honour begins when he asks Lazarillo whether the grimy bread that he has been carrying around "es amasado de manos limpias" (3. 101–2); so does the demonstration of its futility, when, despite Lazarillo's far from encouraging reply (3. 103–4), hunger drives him to eat. Even if one does not believe that the author was a *converso*, it is tempting to see this passage as a satirical comment on the growing concern with *limpieza de sangre* in Old Christian families. From this point onwards, the Squire's insistence on honour ("por lo que toca a mi honra", 3. 266; "no sientes las cosas de la honra", 466–7; "lo que tocaba a mi honra", 502) alternates with Lazarillo's sardonic observations ("la negra que llaman honra", 208–9; "con este mal han de morir", 352; "su negra que dicen honra", 375). There is a surprising outcome: the Squire's view prevails. Lázaro comes to accept that outward appearances are decisive, and after four years with the Chaplain he is able to "me vestir muy honrada-mente de la ropa vieja" (6. 12–13), and even to welcome the Arch-priest's assurance that honour equals profit (7. 47–50).

These themes are, then, interdependent: rising and falling is an aspect of Fortune; adverse Fortune is manifested in hunger, which leads to the theme of struggle and contest. Hypocrisy, illu-sion and honour are a close-knit group, and are linked, through social pretensions and through hypocrisy as a weapon in life's battle, to the theme of rising and falling. The interdependence is structural as well as conceptual: all the themes are mentioned early in the book, and some then disappear, only to return and dominate later sections, sometimes singly, sometimes in conjunction with other themes. This is the technique of interlace (see the end of Ch. 4).

It is much easier to define the themes of *Lazarillo de Tormes* than to establish its author's intentions. It is a commonplace of modern criticism that the discovery of the intentions behind a literary work is a most delicate and difficult task; some critics would say that it is impossible. Even when an author tells us his intentions, he may be remembering wrongly, or may have reasons for misleading us. In *Lazarillo* we are spared this difficulty, only to be faced with worse: we do not know who the author was, so we can obtain no help from external circumstances; and the author has hidden behind his character, the narrator Lázaro, with extreme thoroughness and disconcerting success. We can, of course, ask ourselves what the narrator's intentions are, but we must remem-ber that this is a judgment on a literary character.

Nevertheless, it is in practice impossible to refrain from speculat-ing about the author's intentions. The question "What is the point of this book?" cannot be evaded, and an attempt to answer it is useful, as long as we remember that any conclusions are guesses, and that each reader's guess is likely to differ slightly, or even radically. Some guesses, however, can be supported with a reason-able amount of evidence. First of all, this is a comic book, and at least part of the author's intention must have been to make his readers laugh. This is not only a reasonable deduction from the fact that readers do laugh at many of the incidents (and did in the sixteenth century – the preface to David Rowland's translation refers to "much mirth"); we can in addition observe characters in the story laughing at a number of the incidents.

It is unlikely that the author intended to write a funny book and nothing more, since in that case much of his careful structural and stylistic planning would have been pointless. Most critics see in *Lazarillo* a criticism of society, the caustic depiction of a character's moral evolution, or both.

Social criticism is traditional in European literature: attacks on the abuse of power, on unworthy priests, and in general on those who, at whatever level, betray their function in society. There is also a long tradition of satire as a vehicle for such attacks. Given these facts, one can scarcely imagine that the author was unaware of the amount of social satire in *Lazarillo*. The way in which he presents his criticism is often amusing, but he must, I think, have wanted to draw attention to faults in society, and since most of his victims are clerics, he must have felt strongly about abuses in the Church. The portrait of the Squire makes it fairly clear that the author also wanted to draw attention to the dangers of obsession with social status. It is more difficult to decide his attitude to the "homo novus", and to the poor. His parody of "homo novus" treatises need not imply hostility to the socially mobile, any more than his Biblical parodies imply hostility to Christianity; this may simply have been a vehicle for humour and for the presentation of a character. As for the poor, it is dangerously easy to attribute attitudes we approve of to an author we admire,[3] but even when due caution has been exercised, it does seem likely that the author of *Lazarillo* felt sympathy for them and anger at the way they were treated.

A third element in the author's probable intentions is the depiction of his protagonist's corruption – not merely the final state, but the process of corruption. Whatever view modern critics take of Lázaro, they agree that an innocent child has become a degraded adult. Woodward puts the final corruption at a much earlier stage

[3] As far as I know, nobody has yet claimed the "Coco" joke (1. 36–9) as a protest against racialism, but no doubt someone will.

of Lázaro's life than most critics : for him, the Lazarillo of *Tratado* III is already despicable (*45*). Truman and Jaén, for very different reasons, find much to commend in the adult Lázaro (*40*; *41*; *25*). Most critics agree with Willis (*44*) and Wardropper (*43*) that Lázaro's moral position at the end of the novel is the opposite of that which he reaches in *Tratado* III, and I think that, on the whole, this is correct. At every point along this spectrum of opinions, however, it is clear that an undesirable transformation has occurred in the protagonist. It seems reasonable to go one step further, and conclude that the author wanted us to observe this transformation and to reflect upon it. Several critics have, rightly, pointed out the relevance of the "Coco" joke : if we turn aside in revulsion from the man that Lázaro has become, are we not closing our eyes to potential or actual corruption in ourselves?

These are serious issues, but I do not think they are incompatible with comedy. The great comic writers have generally criticized the societies in which they lived, and they have frequently held strong moral positions. Nor are such issues incompatible with the desire to produce a literary masterpiece. The author of *Lazarillo* did not know that he was writing a novel (see Ch. 10), but it would be strange if he did not, at some stage in the creative process, appreciate the quality of his work and resolve to make it still higher.

I began this discussion of intentions by emphasizing that, whatever is true of literature in general, conclusions about the intentions of *Lazarillo*'s author can only be guesses. I am conscious that what I have said about his intentions is, far from being adventurous and original, a statement of the obvious. To utter platitudes while remaining uneasily aware that one cannot prove their truth is, perhaps, an appropriate fate for any reader of this complex and ambiguous novel.

It is obvious that the author of *Lazarillo de Tormes* did not know that he was writing a picaresque novel, even though his successors in the genre knew that he had written one. Indeed, he can hardly have realized that he was writing a novel at all. Literary criticism as we know it today – a description of a book's distinctive strengths and weaknesses, an assessment of its relation to other works in the same genre, an enquiry into the author's objectives and his degree of success in attaining them – existed only fragmentarily and half accidentally in the sixteenth century. There was no settled tradition of descriptive criticism, and no established critical vocabulary. Even half a century after *Lazarillo*, when Cervantes came to write the first part of *Don Quijote*, he had to base his theoretical approach largely on Aristotle's prescriptions for the epic, and on the sixteenth-century commentators on Aristotle.[1] On the practical side, *Lazarillo*'s author had few novels from which to learn, and the chief of these, *La Celestina*, is atypical, being wholly in dialogue.

What, then, did the author think he was writing? As with the problem of intentions, one can only try to make an informed guess, though in this case a clear statement from the supposed author, Lázaro, would be a valuable guide (there is every reason why we should suspect what Lázaro says about the book's moral, no reason why we should disbelieve him about its purely literary aims). In the Prologue, it is referred to, directly or by implication, as "libro" (*Pr.* 6), "obra" (16), "esta nonada" (28), "pobre servicio" (32), and "entera noticia de mi persona" (36). The first two are much too general, the next two mere *topoi*, but "entera noticia de mi persona" points in the same direction as the title : *La vida de Lazarillo de Tormes y de sus fortunas y adversidades* (since the words are identical in the three editions of 1554, we may assume that they occurred in the lost archetype). This seems, in the author's eyes, to have been a kind of autobiography. A special kind, it is necessary

[1] E. C. Riley, *Cervantes's Theory of the Novel* (Oxford : Clarendon, 1962).

to add, since it is both fictional and parodic, but there was ample precedent for autobiography, for fiction and for parody, even though the words themselves were not in general critical use until much later.

There is one other special feature of which the author must have been well aware. The book incorporates a number of comic incidents, whose humour varies from brutal slapstick to delicate irony. Here too, precedent was readily available: the short comic tale, in various forms, had for centuries been part of the European literary tradition (and in oral tradition must have existed for many thousands of years).[2] The framing of short narratives within a longer one was also a well established tradition. It is possible that the autobiographical form was chosen mainly as a device for assembling and preserving tales which were in danger of extinction, as C. A. Jones suggests (see Ch. 8, note 1), though I think it more likely that the comic episodes were intended to strengthen the author's parody of more elevated forms of biography, of the "homo novus" treatises, and of the chivalresque romances (such a multiplicity of targets is consistent with other complexities and multiple meanings in the novel). In either case, the framework and the individual tales combine to produce what has rightly been called "a masterpiece of comedy . . . one of the funniest books in the language".[3] In this Critical Guide, other aspects have received greater emphasis, since the humour of *Lazarillo* needs less explanation, but we must never forget that the principal reason for the novel's popularity over the centuries is that it has made readers laugh.[4] There is, on the other hand, no conflict between the writing of a comic masterpiece and the wish to make a serious moral point (or even several points). Much of the structural care that went into the book is unnecessary if the author aimed to amuse and nothing more.

Lazarillo's position as a pioneer (the author perhaps resembled "el soldado que es primero del escala", *Pr.* 17–18, more closely than he realized) made a steadily evolving technique natural. *Tratado* I is far more episodic, and more heavily folkloric, than the

---

[2] See *Medieval Comic Tales*, ed. Derek Brewer (Cambridge: Brewer, 1973).

[3] R. O. Jones, *The Golden Age: prose and poetry*, pp. 66–7.

[4] Cf. P. E. Russell, "*Don Quixote* as a Funny Book", *MLR*, LXIV (1969), 312–26.

rest of the book. Physical violence, which is presented as funny, is confined to the first two *tratados*. The comedy of visual exaggeration is found almost exclusively in the first three *tratados*. Imagery is less frequent in the second half of the book, and it would not be difficult to extend this list (see, for example, *10*, pp. 16 and 23–4). It seems probable that the author planned *Tratados* I–III, with their emphasis on hunger and their careful gradation, as a unit, and that when they ended he suffered temporarily from "una especie de fatiga o impotencia creadora" (*26*, p. 154, reverting to the view of *39*, p. 421). Yet the great writer can turn even his creative problems to advantage, and the abrupt change of tempo at the beginning of *Tratado* IV serves to disengage the reader from the immediacy of Lazarillo's experience (*23*, pp. 275–6; *44*, pp. 274–5). From this point onwards, stylistic brilliance and open laughter are less important than irony and the drawing together of the novel's structural and thematic threads.

Finally, we must again remember that the author nowhere makes an appearance in this novel (for the contrary view, see *36*, pp. 7–8). The book is Lázaro-centred to an extraordinary degree: after the first few paragraphs, which name his parents and stepfather, no character apart from Lazarillo himself has a name (*11*, p. ix). The Blind Man, the Priest, the Squire and the rest are labelled according to occupation, rank or other feature; it is as if nobody outside his earliest childhood memories is fully human. Moreover, the autobiographical illusion is flawlessly consistent. Unlike most protagonists of fictional autobiographies, Lázaro tells us nothing that he could not realistically have known, and he distinguishes carefully between what he observed and what he was told (*13*, pp. lxviii–lxix; *35*, pp. 38–9). This is artistically impressive; it is one of the causes of the book's power over its readers; but it is also a source of difficulty. The failure of critics to agree on *Lazarillo*'s meaning is in painful contrast to the wide agreement on its more purely literary aspects. We cannot blame either neglect or ineptitude for this failure: the novel has been widely studied, and has attracted the interest of some of the best scholars and critics in modern hispanism, both in Spain and abroad. Neither can we reasonably blame the author: no writer of this quality is likely to fail, through inadvertence or clumsiness, to tell us what he means.

It may be that the persistent ambiguity of *Lazarillo* is due to moral relativism on the author's part, as Rico suggests (35, pp. 52–5). A more likely explanation, however, is that touched on by Rico in the same essay: that the author's self-effacement leaves us without explicit guidance. Some degree of bewilderment as we read Lázaro's story is the price we have to pay for the book's qualities – the price, as Wayne Booth puts it, of impersonal narration.[5] If an author does not step in to tell us, directly or indirectly, what we should think of his plot and his characters, our reading will be as hard to interpret as our observation of our friends' lives, or even of our own. The story, in short, is about us.

---

[5] *The Rhetoric of Fiction*, Ch. XI–XII. Even in real autobiographies there is something of the same problem: see Roy Pascal, *Design and Truth in Autobiography* (London: Routledge, 1960).

Bibliographical Note

A. BIBLIOGRAPHIES

The most extensive is Joseph L. Laurenti's, in *Annali dell'Istituto Universitario Orientale di Napoli, Sezione Romanza*, 8 (1966), 265-317, with a supplement in 13 (1971), 293-330. Bruno M. Damiani has a useful survey of recent scholarship in 12 (1970), 5-19. American *Lazarillo* criticism is shrewdly and elegantly assessed by Bruce W. Wardropper, in *Modern Literature*, II, ed. Victor Lange, The Princeton Studies: Humanistic Scholarship in America (Englewood Cliffs: Prentice-Hall, 1968), pp.96-98.

B. BACKGROUND

The best historical treatment in English is J.H. Elliott's *Imperial Spain 1469-1716* (London: Arnold, 1963), Ch. 5-6. Elliott deals with the period again in Ch.4 of *Spain: A Companion to Spanish Studies*, ed. P.E. Russell (London: Methuen, 1973). For the literary background, see the two Golden Age volumes of *A Literary History of Spain*, ed. R.O. Jones (London: Benn; New York: Barnes and Noble): Jones, *Prose and Poetry*, and Edward M. Wilson and Duncan Moir, *Drama* (both 1971). A briefer, but also very good, survey is given by P.E. Russell, in Ch.8 of *Spain: A Companion*.

C. THE PICARESQUE NOVEL

1. Del Monte, Alberto, *Itinerario de la novela picaresca española*, trans. Enrique Sordo, Palabra en el Tiempo, 73 (Barcelona: Lumen, 1971). Italian original, 1957; this trans. has been brought up to date. Stresses socio-economic factors (sometimes excessively, but often helpfully). Pp.17-61 on *Lazarillo*.
2. Guillén, Claudio, *Literature as System: Essays toward the Theory of Literary History* (Princeton: Univ. Press, 1971). Contains two major theoretical articles (Ch. 3 and 5) on the picaresque.
3. Miller, Stuart, *The Picaresque Novel* (Cleveland, Ohio: Case Western Reserve Univ. Press, 1967). After *4*, the best critical survey in English.

Divided by features, not by works, so that *Lazarillo* may be compared
with its successors.

4. Parker, Alexander A. *Literature and the Delinquent: The Picaresque
    Novel in Spain and Europe 1599-1753* (Edinburgh: Univ. Press, 1967).
    The best treatment in English (probably in any language), although it
    virtually excludes *Lazarillo*, which is seen as a precursor, not as a
    picaresque novel.
5. Whitbourn, Christine J. 'Moral Ambiguity in the Spanish Picaresque
    Tradition', in *Knaves and Swindlers: Essays on the Picaresque Novel in
    Europe*, ed. Whitbourn (London: Oxford Univ. Press for Univ. of Hull,
    1974), pp.1-24. A sensible and useful comparison of *Lazarillo*'s
    ambiguity with that of its successors.

D. EDITIONS

6. Blecua, Alberto, Clásicos Castalia, 58 (Madrid: Castalia, 1974). An
    excellent critical edition, with introduction and notes of high quality;
    analogues in the notes are especially useful. The introduction gives
    great attention to textual problems.
7. Caso González, José, *Boletin de la Real Academia Española*, anejo 17
    (Madrid: RAE, 1967). Introduction entirely devoted to textual
    problems, with unnecessarily elaborate filiation of early editions.
    Editorial practice is sensible, and variants are copiously listed in notes.
    See Francisco Rico, 'En torno al texto crítico del *LT*', *HR*, 38 (1970),
    405-19.
8. Cavaliere, Alfredo (Napoli: Giannini, 1955). The first of the important
    modern editions. Introduction and notes are chiefly textual.
9. Cejador y Frauca, Julio, Clásicos Castellanos, 25 (Madrid: La Lectura,
    1914). Still widely sold and quoted, but now badly out of date.
10. Guillén, Claudio (with *El Abencerraje*; New York: Dell, 1966). A very
    good student edition, now unfortunately out of print. Excellent intro-
    duction and good notes.
11. Hesse, Everett W., and Harry F. Williams (Madison: Univ. of Wiscon-
    sin Press, 1948, 2nd ed. 1961). Text and notes now superseded by other
    editions, but still interesting for Américo Castro's brief but influential
    introduction (Spanish version in *Hacia Cervantes*, Madrid: Taurus,
    1957).
12. Jones, R.O. (Manchester: Univ. Press, 1963). Very good text, with
    excellent introduction. Notes are chiefly lexical.
13. Rico, Francisco, in *La novela picaresca española*, I, Clásicos Planeta,
    12 (Barcelona: Planeta, 1967, 2nd ed. 1970). Another very good text
    with excellent introduction and notes.

14. Riquer, Martín de, in *La Celestina y Lazarillos* (Barcelona: Vergara, 1959). Few notes, but still valuable for its introduction.

E. CRITICISM

15. Ayala, Francisco, *El Lazarillo: nuevo examen de algunos aspectos*, Cuadernos Taurus, 106 (Madrid: Taurus, 1971). A discursive commentary, with some useful observations and some red herrings.
16. Bataillon, Marcel, *Novedad y fecundidad del LT*, trans. Luis Cortés Vázquez (Salamanca: Anaya, 1968). Trans. of introd. to Paris, 1958 edition of *Lazarillo*; notes brought up to date. Indispensable.
17. Blanquat, Josette, 'Fraude et frustration dans *LT*', in José L. Alonso Hernández *et al.*, *Culture et marginalités au XVIe siècle* (Paris: Klincksieck, 1973), pp.41-73. Shows the importance of these two themes, and makes some useful incidental points. Author has read little recent *Lazarillo* criticism, so seems strangely old-fashioned.
18. Carey, Douglas M., 'Asides and Interiority in *LT*: A Study in Psychological Realism', *Studies in Philology*, 66 (1969), 119-34. A useful and well documented study.
19. Concha, Víctor G[arcía] de la, 'La intención religiosa del *Lazarillo*', *Revista de Filología Española*, 55 (1972), 243-77. An ample collection of religious references, intelligently classified and sensibly discussed.
20. Durand, Frank, 'The Author and Lázaro: Levels of Comic Meaning', *BHS*, 45 (1968), 89-101. A careful and sensitive analysis of humour in the work and of its thematic importance.
21. Gatti, José F., *Introducción al LT* (Buenos Aires: Centro Editor de América Latina, 1968). An unpretentious but sound and well-informed pamphlet, whose only weakness is the extreme brevity of the section on style.
22. Gilman, Stephen, 'The Death of Lazarillo de Tormes', *PMLA*, 81 (1966), 149-66. Packed with acute observations on style, structure and (more debatably) theme.
23. Guillén, Claudio, 'La disposición temporal del *LT*', *HR*, 25 (1957), 264-79. The definitive treatment of the use of time in *Lazarillo*. This article began a brilliant five-year flowering of American *Lazarillo* studies (*37, 43, 44*) which, with the simultaneous *16*, completed the revolution begun by Tarr (*39*) and prepared the way for a new phase of criticism.
24. Hutman, Norma L., 'Universality and Unity in the *LT*', *PMLA*, 76 (1961), 469-73. Based on the discoveries referred to under *23*; adds some interesting points.
25. Jaén, Didier T., 'La ambigüedad moral del *LT*', *PMLA*, 83 (1968), 130-34. More a defence of the adult Lázaro, seen as still charitable, than a study of ambiguity.

26. Lázaro Carreter, Fernando, *LT en la picaresca*, Letras e Ideas, Minor, 1 (Barcelona: Ariel, 1972). Reprints three papers of 1968, including the definitive studies of precedents for autobiographical form and of folklore.

27. Lida de Malkiel, María Rosa, 'Función del cuento popular en el *LT*', in *Actas del I Congreso Internacional de Hispanistas* (Oxford: Dolphin,1964), pp.349-59. The first serious study of folklore in relation to *Lazarillo*'s structure; prepared the ground for 26.

28. Lomax, Derek W., 'On Re-Reading the *LT*', in *Studia iberica: Festschrift für Hans Flasche* (Bern: Francke, 1973), pp.371-81. A provocatively written reassessment, showing that stress on poverty and clerical immorality is due to a revolution of rising expectations. Suggests several layers of criticism.

29. McGrady, Donald, 'Social Irony in *LT* and its Implications for Authorship', *Romance Philology*, 23 (1969-70), 557-67. A new approach to the *converso* problem, sometimes convincing, sometimes tenuous.

30. Mancing, Howard, 'The Deceptiveness of *LT*', *PMLA*, 90 (1975), 426-32. Shows, eloquently and effectively, the difference between Lazarillo and Lázaro, and the effect of this difference on the reader.

31. Minguet, Charles, *Recherches sur les structures narratives dans le LT*, Thèses, Mémoires et Travaux, 15 (Paris: Centre de Recherches Hispaniques, 1970). A structuralist approach, more striking in method than in conclusions; but its tabulation of material is useful, even though it makes some issues seem more clear-cut than they really are.

32. Morreale, Margarita, 'Reflejos de la vida española en el *Lazarillo*', *Clavileño*, no.30 (Nov.-Dec. 1954), 28-31. Presents fascinating analogues to *Lazarillo* situations from Cortes documents; now supplemented by 6.

33. Perry, T. Anthony, 'Biblical Symbolism in the *LT*', *Studies in Philology*, 67 (1970), 139-46. Rightly stresses Biblical as against Jungian patterns, and makes some valid points, but most of the parallels are far-fetched.

34. Rico, Francisco, 'Problemas del *Lazarillo*', *Boletin de la Real Academia Española*, 46 (1966), 277-96. Excellent treatment of 'el caso' and of the Squire. Some overlap with 13 and 35.

35. ——, *La novela picaresca y el punto de vista* (Barcelona: Seix Barral, 1970, 2nd ed. 1973). Ch. 1, '*LT*, o la polisemia', is an original and penetrating study of the book's Lázaro-centred nature. Ch.3 has useful information on the early diffusion of *Lazarillo*.

36. Rumeau, A., *Le LT: essai d'interprétation, essai d'attribution* (Paris: Ediciones Hispano-Americanas, 1964). A brief and vigorous dissenting opinion on several issues. Notably, but unconvincingly, rejects Lázaro as centre of book and asserts author's presence.

37. Sicroff, Albert A., 'Sobre el estilo del *LT*', *NRFH*, 11 (1957), 157-70. Deals with structure as well as style, finding the book's unity flawed. See *23*.

38. Siebenmann, Gustav, *Über Sprache und Stil im 'LT'*, Romanica Helvetica, 43 (Bern: Francke, 1953). A thorough study of the linguistic side of *Lazarillo's* style.

39. Tarr, F. Courtney, 'Literary and Artistic Unity in the *LT*', *PMLA*, 42 (1927), 404-21. The foundation of all serious *Lazarillo* criticism.

40. Truman, R.W., 'Parody and Irony in the Self-Portrayal of Lázaro de Tormes', *MLR*, 63 (1968), 600-05. Raises some disturbing points about the seriousness of Lázaro's narrative.

41. ———, 'Lázaro de Tormes and the *Homo novus* Tradition', *MLR*, 64 (1969), 62-67. Shows that *Lazarillo* is a parody of treatises which praise the virtuous self-made man; important for theme as well as source studies. *42*, which suggests specific sources, is rightly more tentative.

42. ———, '*LT*, Petrarch's *De remediis adversae fortunae*, and Erasmus's *Praise of Folly*', *BHS*, 52 (1975), 33-53. See *41*.

43. Wardropper, Bruce W., 'El trastorno de la moral en el *Lazarillo*', *NRFH*, 15 (1961), 441-47. The classic study of Lazarillo's corruption. See *23*.

44. Willis, Raymond S., 'Lazarillo and the Pardoner: The Artistic Necessity of the Fifth *Tractado*', *HR*, 27 (1959), 267-79. Confronts and resolves the problem of sudden structural change. See *23*.

45. Woodward, L.J., 'Author-Reader Relationship in the *Lazarillo del Tormes*', *Forum for Modern Language Studies*, 1 (1965), 43-53. A rightly influential reaction against over-indulgent views of the protagonist, but sometimes pushes the evidence harder than it will bear.

SUPPLEMENTARY BIBLIOGRAPHY

A. BIBLIOGRAPHIES

46. Morros, Bienvenido C., 'Apéndice bibliográfico', in *60*, pp.147-91. A comprehensive bibliography with a substantial and judicious descriptive introduction. The indispensable starting-point for anyone planning to work on *LT*, though it is marred by printer's errors.

C. THE PICARESQUE NOVEL

47. Bjornson, Richard, *The Picaresque Hero in European Fiction* (Madison: Univ. of Wisconsin Press, 1977). Chap.1 on *LT*.

48. Dunn, Peter N., *The Spanish Picaresque Novel*, Twayne's World Authors Series, 557 (Boston: Twayne, 1979). Chap.2 on *LT* and its continuations.

49. Guillén, Claudio, *The Anatomies of Roguery: A Comparative Study of the Origins and the Nature of Picaresque Literature* (New York: Garland, 1987). His 1953 doctoral thesis, from which a series of highly original and influential publications (*2, 10, 23*) arose.

50. Ife, B.W., *Reading and Fiction in Golden-Age Spain: A Platonist Critique and some Picaresque Replies* (Cambridge: UP, 1985). Pp.92-117 on *LT*'s relation to the literary theory of the period.

51. Iffland, James, 'El pícaro y la imprenta: algunas conjeturas acerca de la génesis de la novela picaresca', in *Actas del IX Congreso de la Asociación Internacional de Hispanistas, 18-23 agosto 1986, Berlín*, ed. Sebastian Neumeister (Frankfurt am Main: Vervuert for AIH, 1989), I, pp.495-506.

52. Maravall, José Antonio, *La literatura picaresca desde la historia social (siglos XVI y XVII)* (Madrid: Taurus, 1986).

53. *La picaresca: orígenes, textos y estructuras: Actas del I Congreso Internacional sobre la Picaresca*, ed. Manuel Criado de Val (Madrid: Fundación Universitaria Española, 1979). A collection of papers of widely varying quality and interest; pp. 349-491 on *LT*.

54. Reed, Helen H., *The Reader in the Picaresque Novel* (London: Tamesis, 1984). Pp.36-52 on *LT*.

55. Rey, Alfonso, 'La novela picaresca y el narrador fidedigno', *HR*, 47 (1979), 55-75.

56. Rico, Francisco, *The Spanish Picaresque Novel and the Point of View*, tr. Charles Davis & Harry Sieber (Cambridge: UP, 1984). A translation of the 3rd ed. of *35*, with additional material.

57. Sieber, Harry, *The Picaresque*, The Critical Idiom, 33 (London: Methuen, 1977). A brief and effective guide to the Spanish origins and the European development of the genre.

58. Villanueva, Darío, 'Narratario y lectores implícitos en la evolución formal de la novela picaresca', in *Estudios en honor a Ricardo Gullón* (Lincoln, NE: Society of Spanish and Spanish-American Studies, 1985), pp.343-67.

D. EDITIONS

59. Ricapito, Joseph V., *Tri-Linear Edition of 'LT' of 1554: Burgos, Alcalá de Henares, Amberes* (Madison: Hispanic Seminary of Medieval Studies, 1987). The complete texts of the three earliest editions, arranged for line-by-line comparison. An essential tool for detailed study of *LT*'s textual history.
60. Rico, Francisco, Letras Hispánicas, 44 (Madrid: Cátedra, 1987). Supersedes *13* and subsequent editions by Rico. A critical edition, with a 120-pp. introduction written afresh for this volume. There are now a number of good editions of *LT*, and a couple of excellent ones, but this latest version of Rico's is the best.

E. CRITICISM

61. Adrados, Francisco R., 'La *Vida de Esopo* y *La vida de LT*', *Revista de Filología Española*, 58 (1976 [1978]), 35-45.
62. Alegre, José María, 'Las mujeres en el *LT*', *Revue Romane*, 16 (1981), 3-21; repr. *Arbor*, no.460 (1984), 23-35.
63. Allen, John J., 'The World View of *LT*', in *Studies in Honor of William C. McCrary* (Lincoln, NE: Society of Spanish and Spanish-American Studies, 1986), pp.35-43. *LT* lacks the pessimism of later Spanish picaresque works.
64. Archer, Robert, 'The Fictional Context of *LT*', *MLR*, 80 (1985), 340-50. Argues that the fictional recipient of Lázaro's narrative is the Archpriest of San Salvador: this is a blackmailing letter.
65. Baader, Horst, 'Zum Problem der Anonymität in der spanischen Literatur des Siglo de Oro', *Romanische Forschungen*, 90 (1978), 388-447. *LT* in the context of anonymous Golden-Age literature and the implications of anonymity for the interpreter.
66. Beverley, John, '*Lazarillo* and Primitive Accumulation: Spain, Capitalism and the Modern Novel', *Bulletin of the Midwest Modern Language Association of America*, 15 (1982), 29-42. A Marxist interpretation that, although over-simplified, makes some interesting points.
67. Brenes Carrillo, Dalai, '*Lazarillo*, *Vlixea* y Anon.' *Boletín de la Biblioteca Menéndez Pelayo*, 63 (1987), 57-104. Proposes Gonzalo Pérez, translator of the *Odyssey* (1550), as author.
68. Brownlee, Marina Scordilis, 'Generic Expansion and Generic Subversion: The Two Continuations of *LT*', *Philological Quarterly*, 61 (1982), 317-27.
69. Carey, Douglas M., '*LT* and the Quest for Authority', *PMLA*, 94 (1979), 36-46.

70. Cervigni, Dino S., '*LT* and the *Vita* of Benvenuto Cellini: An Inquiry into Prose Narrative and Genre', *Kentucky Romance Quarterly*, 27 (1980), 373-89.

71. Chevalier, Maxime, 'El problema del éxito de *Lazarillo*', in his *Lectura y lectores en la España de los siglos XVI y XVII* (Madrid: Turner, 1976), pp.167-97.

72. ——, 'Des contes au roman: l'éducation de Lazarille', *Bulletin Hispanique*, 81 (1979), 189-99.

73. Combet, L., 'Contribution à l'analyse structurelle du *LT*: l'épisode de la grappe de raisin', *LNL*, no.217 (1976), 37-49.

74. Cros, Edmond, 'Semántica y estructuras sociales en el *LT*', *Revista Hispánica Moderna*, 39 (1976-77), 79-84.

75. ——, & Antonio Gómez-Moriana, *Lecture idéologique du 'LT'*, Co-Textes, 8 (Montpellier: Centre d'Études et de Recherches Sociocritiques, 1985). Contains Cros on folkloric elements (pp.5-20) and the ideological basis of *LT*'s epistolary form (pp.105-15); Gómez-Moriana on 'La subversión del discurso ritual' (pp. 21-79) and *LT* as a confession made for an Inquisition tribunal (pp.81-103).

76. Cruz, Anne J., '*LT* as Social Redemptor', in *Marginated Groups in Spanish and Portuguese History*, ed. William D. Phillips & Carla Rahn Phillips (Minneapolis: Society for Spanish and Portuguese Historical Studies, 1989), pp.61-69.

77. Davey, E.R., 'The Concept of Man in *LT*', *MLR*, 72 (1977), 597-604.

78. Dehennin, Elsa, '*LT* comme parole de discours et parole de récit', *LNL*, no.217 (1977), 12-56.

79. Dunn, Peter N., '*LT*: The Case of the Purloined Letter', *Revista de Estudios Hispánicos* (USA), 22 (1988), 1-14. Considers what the text's presentation as a confessional letter implies.

80. ——, 'Reading the Text of *LT*', in *Studies in Honor of Bruce W. Wardropper* (Newark, DE: Juan de la Cuesta, 1989), pp.91-104. Shows how changes in reading practice have revealed puzzling elements in the text, and questions some of the commonplaces of *LT* criticism.

81. Ferrer Chivite, Manuel, 'Sustratos conversos en la creación de Lázaro de Tormes', *NRFH*, 33 (1984), 352-79.

82. Fiore, Robert L., *LT*, Twayne's World Authors Series, 714 (Boston: Twayne, 1984). A guide to the work for non-specialist readers that also has a good deal of interest to specialists.

83. Frenk (Alatorre), Margit, 'Tiempo y narrador en el *Lazarillo*: episodio del ciego', *NRFH*, 24 (1975), 197-218.

84. ——, '*LT*: autor, narrador, personaje', in *Romancia europaea et americana: Festschrift für Harri Meier, 8 Januar 1980* (Bonn: Bouvier Verlag Herbert Grundmann, 1980), pp.185-92.

85. ——, 'La ley de tres en el *LT*', in *Homenaje a José Manuel Blecua* (Madrid: Gredos, 1985), pp.193-202. The application of Axel Olrik's 'Law of Three' (see p.35, above).

86. Friedman, Edward H., 'Chaos Restored: Authorial Control and Ambiguity in *LT*', *Crítica Hispánica*, 3 (1981), 59-73.

87. García de la Concha, Víctor, *Nueva lectura del 'Lazarillo': el deleite de la perspectiva*, Literatura y Sociedad, 28 (Madrid: Castalia, 1981). A critical survey of recent studies is the starting-point for essays on 'el caso', *LT*'s epistolary form and its structure, social background, point of view, and linguistic perspectivism. Stresses the work's radical and deliberate ambiguity.

88. Hanrahan, Thomas, '*LT*: Erasmian Satire or Protestant Reform?', *Hispania* (USA), 66 (1983), 333-39. Decides in favour of the latter.

89. Herrero, Javier, 'The Ending of *Lazarillo*: The Wine against the Water', *MLN*, 93 (1978), 313-19. On the parodic use of religious symbolism to mark major changes in the plot.

90. ——, 'The Great Icons of the *Lazarillo*: The Bull, the Wine, the Sausage and the Turnip', *Ideologies & Literature*, no.5 (Jan.-Feb. 1978), 3-18. A symbolic interpretation that owes a good deal to Freudian method.

91. ——, 'Renaissance Poverty and Lazarillo's Family: The Birth of the Picaresque Genre', *PMLA*, 94 (1979), 876-86.

92. Hughes, Gethin, '*LT*: The Fifth *Tratado*', *Hispanófila*, no. 61 (Sep. 1977), 1-9.

93. Martínez Mata, Emilio, 'Notas sobre realismo y verosimilitud literaria en el *LT*' *Archivum*, 34-35 (1984-85), 105-17.

94. Nepaulsingh, Colbert I., 'Lázaro's Fortune', *Romance Notes*, 20 (1979-80), 417-23. Sees the adult Lázaro not as a hypocrite but as someone who tries to defend himself and fails.

95. O'Reilly, Terence, 'The Erasmianism of *LT*', in *Essays in Honour of Robert Brian Tate* (Nottingham: Dept of Spanish, Univ. of Nottingham, 1984), pp.91-100.

96. ——, 'Discontinuity in *LT*: The Problem of *Tratado* Five', *Journal of Hispanic Philology*, 10 (1985-86), 141-49. Argues that the author interpolated the fifth *tratado* into his earlier work without making sure that it fitted.

97. Read, Malcolm K., *The Birth and Death of Language: Spanish Literature and Linguistics 1300-1700* (Potomac, MD: Studia Humanitatis, 1983), pp.103-05, 108-11, and 117-19. Partly psychoanalytic, partly social approach to use of language in *LT*.

98. Redondo, Augustin, 'Pauperismo y mendicidad en Toledo en la época del *Lazarillo*', in *Hommage des hispanistes français à Noël Salomon* (Barcelona: Société des Hispanistes Français & Laia, 1979), pp.703-24.

99. ——, 'Folklore y literatura en el *LT*: un planteamiento nuevo: el "caso" de los tres primeros tratados', in *Mitos, folklore y literatura*, ed. Aurora Egido (Zaragoza: Caja de Ahorros, 1987), pp.79-110.

100. Rico, Francisco, *Problemas del 'Lazarillo'* (Madrid: Cátedra, 1988). Collects nine studies published between 1966 and 1987, including *34*. The principal topics covered are textual history and genre.

101. ——, '*LT*: la invención de la novela', in his *Breve biblioteca de autores españoles* (Barcelona: Seix Barral, 1990), pp.109-19.

102. Rodríguez-Puértolas, Julio, '*LT* o la desmitificación del imperio', in his *Historia, literatura, alienación* (Barcelona: Labor, 1976), pp.173-99. A salutary emphasis on social criticism, but overlooks the medieval sermon tradition.

103. Ruffinatto, Aldo, *Struttura e significazione del 'LT'*. I: *La costruzione del modello operativo; dall'intreccio alla 'fabula'* (Torino: Giappichelli, 1975). II: *La 'fabula'; il modello trasformazionale* (1977). A semiotic analysis of 'microsequenze' and a structuralist analysis of 'macrosequenze', based on a variety of theoretical models. Vol.II ends with Angelo Morino's essay, 'Il discorso carnevalesco del *LT*', pp.147-93, an interesting application of Mikhail Bakhtin's concept of Carnival.

104. ——, 'La parodia como juego de espejos en el *Lazarillo*', in his *Sobre textos y mundos: ensayos de filología y semiótica hispánicas*, tr. José Muñoz Rivas (Murcia: Universidad, 1989), pp.91-112.

105. Sabat de Rivers, Georgina, 'La moral que Lázaro nos propone', *MLN*, 95 (1980), 233-51. Stresses the contrast between the protagonist's life and his literary aspirations.

106 Shipley, George A., 'A Case of Functional Obscurity: The Master Tambourine-Painter of *Lazarillo*, *Tratado* VI', *MLN*, 97 (1982), 225-53. The first of a series of articles that prepare the way for an important and controversial book, finding sexual innuendo in the description of Lázaro's masters' trades, and emphasizing the cynical humour in the protagonist's narration and the element of mutual exploitation.

107. ——, 'The Critic as Witness for the Prosecution: Making the Case against Lázaro de Tormes', *PMLA*, 97 (1982), 179-94.

108. ——, 'The Critic as Witness for the Prosecution: Resting the Case against Lázaro de Tormes', in *Creation and Re-Creation: Experiments in Literary Form in Early Modern Spain: Studies in Honor of Stephen Gilman* (Newark, DE: Juan de la Cuesta, 1983), pp.105-24.

109. ——, 'Lázaro and the Cathedral Chaplain: A Conspirational Reading of *LT*, *Tratado* VI', *Symposium*, 37 (1983), 216-41.

110. ——, '*LT* Was Not a Hardworking, Clean-Living Water Carrier', in *Hispanic Studies in Honor of Alan D. Deyermond: A North American Tribute* (Madison: Hispanic Seminary of Medieval Studies, 1986), pp.247-55.

111. Sieber, Harry, *Language and Society in 'La vida de LT'* (Baltimore: Johns Hopkins UP, 1978 [1979]). Drawing on semiotics and on psychoanalytic theory, studies the social implications and consequences of language in Lázaro's relations with his masters and in his communication with Vuestra Merced.

112. Smith, Paul Julian, *Writing in the Margin: Spanish Literature of the Golden Age* (Oxford: Clarendon Press, 1988), pp.89-99. An application of some recent literary theories; see pp.6-7, above.

113. Thompson, B. Bussell, & J.K. Walsh, 'The Mercedarian's Shoes: Perambulations on the Fourth *Tratado* of *LT'*, *MLN*, 103 (1988), 440-48.

114. Vilanova, Antonio, *Erasmo y Cervantes*, Palabra Crítica, 8 (Barcelona: Lumen, 1989), pp.126-325. Collects six articles, published between 1978 and 1986; three are on Apuleius, *The Golden Ass*, as a source of *LT*, two are on the character of Lázaro, and one on Erasmian sources for the Squire.

115. Waley, Pamela, *'Lazarillo*'s Cast of Thousands, or the Ethics of Poverty', *MLR*, 83 (1988), 591-601. Argues that, given the circumstances of Lázaro's life, he is good, like most of the people he meets.

116. Wardropper, Bruce W., 'The Strange Case of Lázaro Gonzales Pérez', *MLN*, 92 (1977), 202-12. No longer holding the views expressed in *43*, Wardropper sees *LT* as an ironic expansion of the parable of the rich man and Lazarus (Luke 16: 19-31): a cynical novel without a clear message.

117. ——, 'The Implications of Hypocrisy in the *LT'*, in *Studies in Honor of Everett W. Hesse* (Lincoln, NE: Society of Spanish and Spanish-American Studies, 1981), pp.179-86.

118. Woods, M.J., 'Pitfalls for the Moralizer in *LT'*, *MLR*, 74 (1979), 590-98. Sees readers as trapped by the text into making moral judgments that are later shown to be untenable.

119. Woodward, L.J., 'Le *Lazarillo*: oeuvre d'imagination ou document social?', *Théorie et pratique politiques à la Renaissance: XVII Colloque International de Tours* (Paris: J. Vrin, 1977), pp.333-47.

120. Zappala, Michael, 'The *Lazarillo*: Source — Apuleius or Lucian? — and Recreation', *Hispanófila*, no.97 (Sep. 1989), 1-16. Maintains that Lucian is the more likely.

CRITICAL GUIDES TO SPANISH TEXTS

Edited by
J.E. Varey, A.D. Deyermond and C. Davies

CRITICAL GUIDES TO SPANISH TEXTS

Edited by
J.E. Varey, A.D. Deyermond and C. Davies